THE SHIP

*We are standing upon the seashore... A ship
Spreads her white sails to the morning breeze, and
Starts for the blue ocean. She is an object of beauty
And strength and I stand and watch her until at
Length she is only a ribbon of white cloud just where
The sea and sky come to mingle with each other.
Then someone at my side says, "There! She's Gone!"
Gone Where?*

CLOSER
Than We Imagine

BY

RICHARD M. WAINWRIGHT

To Kathy
"Love is forever!"
Best wishes always —
Your friend,
Dick
Richard M. Wainwright
2004
from Suzanne
with love!

Published by Family Life Publishing

FAMILY LIFE
PUBLISHING

Published by Family Life Publishing
Text copyright © Richard M. Wainwright
Cover Illustration copyright © Ron Walotsky
Photography: Linda Martin and Peggy Mantz
Graphic Design: Mary Sellner Orr

For information write:
Richard M. Wainwright Books / Family Life Publishing
December to June   July to November
Box 353844   87 Rebecca Road
Palm Coast, FL 32135   Scituate, MA 02066
1-800-633-1357

www.rmwainwrightbooks.com

Publisher's Cataloging-in-Publication
Wainwright, Richard M.
Closer than we imagine / Richard M. Wainwright
1st ed.* P.cm.
Includes bibliographical references.
ISBN: 1-928976-02-6
1. Wainwright, Richard M. - Religion.
2. Spiritual biography.   3. Widowers-Biography.   4 Future life.
I Title.BL73.W35A32001   291.4'092 [B]
QBI00-500169
Printed in the United States of America
RICHARD M. WAINWRIGHT BOOKS
Family Life Publishing
First American Edition, July 2001

10 9 8 7 6 5 4 3 2 1

FOREWARD

CLOSER THAN WE IMAGINE is a book Richard never expected to write, never wanted to write, but one that he finally came to believe he must write.

Richard's childhood and early adult years were full of life's lessons: some sad, some happy but all leading to emotional growth. As a young adult he was fortunate to meet a woman who became his partner and whose love, encouragement and support created a joyous team. A team which tried to do their bit in helping others on their journey as well as joining all who strive to make our world a better place.

Richard and D'Ann's life together was blessed. They had a stable marriage with many family and friends deeply interwoven into their thirty-three years of married life. They were looking forward to slowing down after Richard's eighth book, which was to be published in 1996. They planned to spend more time in Florida and do many things they had mentally saved for retirement. On August 1,1995 D'Ann was diagnosed with uterine cancer. She died a little over four months later on December 18th.

After the passing of his beloved wife, Richard's four-year spiritual journey, including some amazing and wonderful experiences, changed him from a skeptical, despairing agnostic to a firm believer in the hereafter. In this special book he simply offers to share these experiences with the reader, hoping his words may bring some comfort and hope to those who have been physically separated from loved ones. The events, which have unfolded since D'Ann's passing, according to Richard, have provided more than sufficient evidence that our spiritual life is never ending. We will see our loved ones again.

You will not forget Richard's story.

Ken Brynildsen

READERS COMMENTS

"The message in this book will impact the lives of all who read it and be of help to them at some point in time."

DON AND BRENDA LUMDSEN

"I have faced death many times: loved ones, friends, and almost daily in my nursing career. The three things that I have found that we all need are Faith, Family, and Friends. Richard's story shows the strength of all three. Ernest Becker, in many writings on death, states that, without faith of some sort, none of us can face death.

Richard's journey, and his courage in sharing that journey with us, is in itself, spiritual. This book is a gift to all who read it and will serve as a vehicle to help many other people."

KAY WALSH

"We certainly admire you for creating **CLOSER THAN WE IMAGINE** *which is an extraordinary account of your and D'Ann's life together and of the revelation to you of the possibility of a nearby hereafter. It takes guts to expose one's private beliefs to the often times not so agreeable reactions of a readership of strangers, each with his/her degree of beliefs ranging from empathy to complete rejection. You leave us pondering and wondering . . ."*

GORDON AND MADELINE HAMERSLEY

"It was an unexpected pleasure to have been given the privilege of reading the manuscript of this poignant revelation of Richard's dealing with the loss of his beloved wife. D'Ann enriched the life of everyone she touched. It is wonderful to see the remarkable, positive change this writing has made in Richard's life."

JAYNE AND PHILIP LUNDELL

"Thank you for sharing your experience with us. My heart broke the day I heard D'Ann died, I always felt so close to her. The interpretation of messages is comforting to anyone who has lost a loved one."

JULIENNE LENTZ

"You have set yourself a difficult task, because when one believes something passionately, it is tough not to try to sell others. But I think you have succeeded admirably in doing just that! You have put your beliefs in front of the public openly and honestly but without proselytizing. If you spoke in milder terms, one might question whether or not you yourself believed in what you are saying. Certainly the book will stir some discussion and debate, but if it didn't, you wouldn't have had much to say. I wouldn't change a word."

PETE SCOTT

*"Your thoughts on the hereafter are beautifully shared
with your readers and your readers are going to be left
with a feeling of hope. Your message on how we love is especially
important for us to hear at any time in life."*

CAROLYN PAYNE

*"Wow!! An integral part of my talks on reading aloud is a discussion
of what makes a book "literature." I contend that,
for one thing, literature makes the reader laugh, cry, or think.
The storm of thoughts and emotional reactions I experienced in
reading* **CLOSER THAN WE IMAGINE** *mark it as true literature.*

*I remain what you refer to as an 'honorary Missourian': maybe even
St. Thomas' brother . . . Your descriptions made everything a lot more
believable. They also caused me to feel truly joyous. Thank you for
having the courage to write such a self-revealing book."*

BRENDON WALSH, PH.D.

*"The enlightened spiritual human being shows four
characteristics: ethical and moral elevation, compassion for all and
service to mankind, unique and genius like expressive abilities, and
expansion of consciousness to the point of superconscious experience.*

*Let the reader decide as Richard unfolds his wonderful,
poignant and beautiful spiritual journey."*

HEBER KIMBALL, PH.D.

*"What a beautiful story. I'm so glad you decided to write it.
I'm sure it will serve to validate many people's experiences of
communications with their loved ones who have moved through the
portal we call death. I'm always teaching, "Death is simply the name
we've given to the doorway back to the creator: back to love.*

*Your intimate sharing of your discoveries on your path of love and
healing show a great caring for your fellow man. To take the risk of
baring an inner part of our soul to those we know is an act
of calculated risk: to bare our soul to those we have not met
is an act of love, compassion, and bravery."*

BONNIE BURROWS

*"I remember thinking that it was too late at night to read these pages,
until I began to glance at them, then I couldn't put them down.*

*Richard puts down in black and white what
a lot of ordinary people like me think about the
actual 'being-ness' of loved ones we have lost, after they
have been buried. One can only hope that those
special close feelings of communication, which come out of the blue,
could actually BE a communication with a loved one.
I admire his willingness to share with us such deep personal revelations.
They will be of great comfort to many of us.
I plan to tell everyone about this book."*

KATHLEEN TIBERII

*"I have often told others that if you read one of Richard's books,
you will want to read everything he has written.
Although **CLOSER THAN WE IMAGINE** is for adults,
it is equally as mesmerizing as his other titles.*

*Richard's wife, D'Ann, was one of my dearest friends.
Her passing was a great loss to all who knew and loved her.
Yet, having had a near death experience years ago,
I believe that we return to the light and a loving afterlife.
Richard's spiritual journey included two remarkable meetings
with George Anderson, which not only convinced Richard
that one day each of us will be reunited with our loved ones,
but also, that there are many reasons why we should
do our best to live a caring and productive life.
You will want to share Richard's story."*

LOIS WOODWARD

*"Thank you for your courage to write
CLOSER THAN WE IMAGINE . . . a story written
from the heart. As one who has had a near-death experience,
one who works as a Hospice volunteer, and is a member
of The Bereavement Ministry team at our church,
this is the book I have been waiting for!
It will be an honor for me to share your gentle
messages of love, hope, comfort, and joy!"*

PENNY WIGGLESWORTH

"When D'Ann died I placed her
oldest and most dearly loved
Teddy Bear beside her
to accompany her
on her final journey."

RMW

"I hope one day we meet up with all lost Teddy Bears again –
and the little lost cats.
And the grandads and grandmas.
What a hugging that will be."

HELEN THOMPSON

b. 1943

D E D I C A T I O N

To D'Ann, Judy, and to all our loved ones,
yours and mine,
past, present, and future.

My sincere thanks to friends and family who proofread my manuscript and contributed their thoughts and encouragement. Special thanks to Ken Brynildsen, good friend, talented writer, and kindred soul whose editing improved my efforts and brought us closer as we traveled this journey together.

I shall forever be grateful to George Anderson for sharing his gift with me.

There will never be a book created which could have enough pages for anyone to recognize all those who have positively influenced their lives. I, too, owe a great debt to countless fellow travelers: my parents, family, friends, masters, students, and even those in the shadows I barely discerned as well as the giants of history. To all those souls whose words and actions have touched my life, my eternal thanks.

Richard

"God bless us everyone!" said Tiny Tim.

CHARLES DICKENS

PROLOGUE

Reading and writing have always been a big part of my life. The Hardy Boys were my brothers, I floated down the Mississippi with Huck Finn, climbed Annapurna with Herzog, and flew with Amelia Earhart. Vicariously, I lived the lives of many great men and women of history and fiction.

Writing gave me the opportunity to use my imagination and experiences to create adventures, people, and places. Who can remember the day our scribbling was declared a WORD by our proud parents? Not I. Eventually we learned to string enough letters together so our intent was no longer a mystery to our teachers and family. Thousands of sentences later, my first book, *A TINY MIRACLE*, was born. Its genesis came from early childhood experiences and of course, my imagination. I tried to write a story for people of all ages rather than just for children. My first literary attempt took several years to write and illustrate. Much to my surprise the book turned into a big miracle for D'Ann and myself.

All my books, I hope, gently focus on universal values, human frailties, strengths, and life's lessons. I have written equally with my heart as with my mind. I am very grateful that my literary efforts and the talents of my wonderful illustrators have been well received by youngsters and adults.

This is one book I did not in any way anticipate writing, ever imagine I would write, or want to write. It has been written because my heart said I must.

I have always believed that loving and sharing are the most important aspects of our existence and possibly the reason for it. My experiences following D'Ann's death have erased my life-long doubts that life continues in another dimension.

I am not a theologian. I have no special psychic gifts. I can be fooled. I am capable of wishful thinking. Yet, because of my experiences during the past four years, I am convinced that our lives continue after death. Our loved ones wait for us in another dimension. Each reader must come to his or her own conclusion regarding the credibility and significance, if any, of my experiences and words. This book is not fiction. It is simply the relating of one human being's spiritual journey, which brought him comfort, hope, and peace.

"Guess now who holds thee?"—
"Death," I said.—But there
The silver answer rang,—"Not Death,
but love."

ELIZABETH BARRETT BROWNING

"There are more things in heaven and
earth, Horatio,
Than are dreamt of in your philosophy."

WILLIAM SHAKESPEARE

When I first thought about writing this book, I laughed at myself. I didn't think it was a very bright idea and, in fact, it was probably a very foolish one. Who would believe it? It would merely confirm what a lot of friends have surmised for years. "Richard's elevator no longer goes to the top floor, he's gone round the bend, It's sad senility coming to him so young."

I felt that proposing we pass to another dimension upon death would put me in the same league as people who report UFO's flying over Cape Cod or claim to be the reincarnation of some great hero or heroine of history. In fact, I think if I claimed to be related by blood to the second cousin, twice removed, to the first mate who told Columbus that India was in sight, I might, just might, at least get sympathy for being delusional or from those most kind, "it's possible." However, since risk-taking has been my strongest suit and major weakness, I place my ordinary life and a few extraordinary experiences in your hands.

"Children and fooles cannot lye."

JOHN HEYWOOD

"We (that's my ship and I) took off rather suddenly.
We had a report somewhere around 4 o'clock in the afternoon
before that the weather would be fine,
so we thought we would try it."

LINDBERGH'S OWN STORY
[of his Non-stop flight, Long Island to Paris],
in *The New York Times*, May 23,1927

"I saw a fleet of fishing boats . . .
I flew down almost touching the craft and yelled at them,
asking if I was on the right road to Ireland.
They just stared. Maybe they didn't hear me.
Maybe I didn't hear them. Or maybe they thought
I was just a crazy fool. An hour later I saw land."

CHARLES AUGUSTUS LINDBERGH

"Life is a great surprise. I do not see why death should not be even greater."

VLADMIR NABOKOV

No, No, No!

$\mathcal{C}h a p t e r$ I

"**Y**our wife has advanced uterine cancer." Those words, like bullets, tore into my heart and I died. The world around me disintegrated—our future vanished. Like a dropped mirror, our dreams lay shattered at my feet.

For the next four months I functioned, lucid, yet in a non-believing state, doing what I had to do to care for D'Ann and at the same time trying to find a treatment that would hold out hope for a cure. Together, we tried to convince each other that we would win this battle. Alone, I cried. I knew we were losing. Later, I learned D'Ann had known too but she had played the game for me. I learned the meaning of despair. I cursed our fate and God for D'Ann's suffering and my quickly approaching loss.

Although I could not see through the veil of tears as I watched D'Ann die a little each day, another stage of my spiritual journey had begun.

ANCIENT HISTORY

Dear reader,

I think it is only fair to warn you that the first section of this book relates to my rather ordinary life before D'Ann so if you are in a hurry you won't miss much by skipping this chapter.

Richard

$\mathcal{C}hapter$ II

I have no idea what I was doing before August 21, 1935, but that was the day I was born. For my parents, Bertha Hicks Wainwright and Edwin Mallard Wainwright, this was a special day too. I was their first born. Unlike today's moms and their babies, my mother and I spent close to a week in the Newton-Wellesley Hospital before we were allowed to go home. Of course, my proud father was nervously waiting to drive us to Nana Whalen's home where my folks were living. Dad often smoked two packs of cigarettes a day, but according to my Aunt Marion, as my mother and I were being wheeled to our very used car, Dad stated in no uncertain terms that there would be no smoking during the trip home. It probably was one of the longest rides of his life.

During my first couple of years of life, my parents' pediatrician told them that I appeared rather frail and predicted an uncertain future. When exposed to a bug, I usually caught it. It seemed to my parents that most childhood diseases known to man dominated my early years. After whooping cough, mumps, measles, pneumonia, and assorted infections, my folks were advised I'd be lucky to live to get a driver's license. As I write, I'm looking forward to my 65th birthday—so much for medical predictions.

My first exposure to religion came when I was led down to the basement of Christ Episcopal Church in Needham, Massachusetts for Sunday school. Friends can remember specific lessons or events during their Sunday school days. They recall their teachers' personalities, looks, and their idiosyncrasies. I don't. I have just a vague memory of volunteer parents (who were earning heavenly points) trying to convey the moral, ethical, and chiseled-in-stone tenets of our particular creed into tiny uninterested toddlers and questioning teens. If anyone deserves a free pass through the pearly gates—they do. Looking back, I guess they did convince me that God had created a beautiful world with a pretty logical and compassionate way of life. I definitely bought His ethical plan.

As a wee lad in Needham, the undeveloped acres outnumbered the mailboxes at least five to one. That day is long gone. Yet memories of weekly adventures exploring the woods, climbing the huge boulders in the High Rock section, or sitting quietly on a blanket of green moss by the ubiquitous bubbling brook, still remain. There, I would spend hours watching water bugs doing their crazy dance. Motionless, I would observe frogs, moles, ants, butterflies, darning needles, and a myriad of insects and small animals pursuing their daily goal of surviving one more day. The complexity, grandeur, beauty, and downright magic of the natural world held me spellbound for hours. The power of the Creator to make such diversity was not lost on my young mind.

My love of nature came from Dad who was one of the gentlest people I ever met. He loved his family, all animals, and any form of life. He raised his last batch of chickens in our backyard on Lewis Street. All fourteen chickens had names and when he would let them out, Matilda, Gertrude, Gloria, Jennifer, etc., would follow him around like a litter of puppies. Dad had a pair of Chilean chickens which supposedly laid colored eggs. For over two years, Dad would look in their nest in vain. The morning after Dad died, Mom found two greenish-blue eggs in their nest. I always wondered about this gift to Mom. She had them blown out and kept them in an egg cozy for years.

Of course, Dad loved his wife, Bee, and his four children, Nancy, Sue, Bob, and me, very, very much. Maybe too much, as the chore of disciplining his brood, went by default to my mother.

In the church choir, I was one of several towheaded blond sopranos with uncontrollable locks. In my black and white cassock,

I looked like an all-American boy angel. The angel bit was left at the church. At home, my mother would tell you I was the epitome of the "terrible twos", cantankerous threes, full of mischief fours, etc., and spoiled rotten by my parents until my siblings began to appear.

Sometime in my early years, I latched on to the silly idea that one should never lose a contest, whether it is getting your own way or winning on the basketball court. Needless to say, this attitude guaranteed lots of problems. Temper tantrums were frequent and later, after an athletic defeat, be it hoops, baseball, or tennis, slammed doors and moping equally got under the skin of those who by blood had to live with me.

Sadly, I never got to know my grandmothers well. (My grandfathers had passed away before I arrived.) I remember Nana Whalen as an old, wrinkled, rather bent, crippled lady with a perpetual smile and twinkle in her eyes, which always seemed to radiate more love than the room could hold. I'll never forget our last visit to see her. On our wedding day, D'Ann and I went directly from the church to her hospital bed. When she saw us in our wedding attire, she seemed to envelop us in love with just her eyes. You could feel the joy our visit had brought her. I never will forget that wonderful moment and her loving face.

Grandma Wainwright was a little reserved. My fondest memory of this spry, white haired lady was sitting in her lap and rocking back and forth as she sang, "Grass Hopper Green is a jolly old chap, he lives . . . "

Just before I became a teen, I was given the honor of carrying the crucifix at the adult Sunday service. I would closely follow our kindly minister down the aisle leading the adult choir. After several uneventful Sundays, my awkward years made a dramatic entrance. I tripped, just missing skewering our Reverend Harry Hall. Although the top point of the cross was not rapier sharp, everyone realized how close I had come to sending our spiritual leader to the hospital. My unintentional lunge would have ruined his and the congregation's day. Wiser heads promoted (or demoted) me to serving as an altar boy.

During high school, there was the Young People's Fellowship. I recall it as a social night out. Occasionally some interesting subject stimulated heated discussions regarding the theology of the Episcopal Church. Most of the time we focused on sports and the opposite sex.

Between five and eighteen it sank in that Episcopalians were not the only members of the human race who went to church on Sundays. There were others in the world that even went to church on Fridays and Saturdays. And there were many in the world who had never read or seen a Bible, who called God another name, and a dwindling number of people remained who believed a pantheon of spirits watched over them. As I read and observed, I learned millions of non-Episcopalians were good people leading moral, caring, and loving lives.

The study of different religions began to erode my certainty that our church had the only right theological answers. In high school, I had the good fortune to become friends with young people who came from diverse ethnic, racial, and economic backgrounds. I also came to know girls and boys who were struggling to achieve even though living with serious physical disabilities. My younger brother, Bob, courageously battled epilepsy with its frequent grand-mal seizures every day of his life. Blind students, deaf students, paralyzed students, those with birth defects, all seemed to rise above their challenges and smile and laugh with those of us who had been so lucky to be born reasonably intact and healthy. Each handicapped person seemed to be able to do more with less than I ever could. They appeared to embrace life to the fullest of their ability without any self-pity. I constantly shook my head in wonder and appreciation when I saw them.

Yet, possibly because my parents lived what they preached, I developed one unshakeable idea that there is a little bit of God in each and every one of us. Mom would see to it the family would get to church at least a few times a year because she felt it was the right thing to do but it was obvious she had her doubts about all the proclaimed truths during these sporadic visits. Yet, her heart was always in the right place. She and my dad personified love and kindness. Their theology was embodied in a poem we heard often.

I expect to pass through this
world but once.
If therefore, there be any kindness
I can show,
or any good thing I can do,
let me do it now;
let me not defer or neglect it
for I shall not pass this way again.

EDWARD COURTENAY
The Earl of Devon

I always felt I knew what was the right thing to do in my heart even though I could justify not doing it. I read of individuals who devoted their lives to caring for and serving others and, of course, the thousands who sacrificed their lives so that my family and I might live in peace. I could see God at work in hundreds of people, yet I couldn't understand His philosophy in populating this planet. There seemed to me to be too many human tragedies that He should have been able to foresee or eliminate.

Why should people hunger in a world with abundant resources? Why are there incurable diseases, accidental and tragic deaths? Why retardation, congenital defects, etc.? Why was my brother born with epilepsy and given only a short life? No matter where I looked for answers to these questions, I came up empty. How could I fully accept a God, which permitted misery for so many? I embraced the good He encouraged, but why He allowed so many innocent people to suffer or tolerated human failings was beyond my comprehension.

When I was fifteen, I received a two-month scholarship to a canoeing camp, Keewaydin, on Lake Dunmore in Vermont. Keewaydin was founded in the 1890's and is now the oldest camp in the United States. Its values and reverence for all life played a big role in shaping my life's philosophy.

My camp counselor was a young man by the name of Johnny McPhee. Johnny was one of the original Princeton Whiz Kids that played Twenty Questions on national radio for many years. Later in life he became a well-known writer with several of his books making the best seller list. I believe his bi-monthly letters to my parents helped hone his literary skills, as they must have been a real challenge to write. My first summer at Keewaydin, Johnny reported as diplomatically as possible that, although I was a decent athlete, and basically got along with everyone, I really hadn't accepted the camp's creed, "help the other fellow."

Fortunately, the staff thought I wasn't a hopeless project and I was invited back for one more year. Shortly after our arrival that summer, the sixteen oldest kids at the camp embarked on a three-week canoe trip to the wilds of northern Maine. It was raining as we made the traditional paddle across Lake Dunmore to waiting trucks which could haul our canoes. It rained steadily nineteen of the next twenty-one days.

After paddling six hours the first day in rain, we set up our tents in a downpour. My fellow trippers wanted dry clothes and a hot meal. It was no fun for anyone, especially the two counselors who felt equally beat. My fellow teenagers waited like birds in a nest for their supper. All that could be heard was the constant drumming of the rain and the grumbling of campers. For some reason, still unknown to me, I kept my mouth shut, crawled out of my tent, and volunteered to help the beleaguered staff. I ferried hot cocoa from tent to tent, and encouraged my compatriots to get into dry clothes A.S.A.P. By the end of the evening, I was the acknowledged third counselor.

By the time we returned to the base camp in Vermont, I had grown up. Thankfully, Johnny McPhee was able to write my parents that a metamorphosis had taken place. Their son might turn out to be a decent human being after all. (My mother saved those letters for years and I believe she took them out to read whenever I had relapses later in my life.)

In high school, having majored in athletics, girls, and cafeteria, my academic achievements were spotty at best. If I was to gain admission to a good college, a post graduate year of prep school was recommended. Although I worked summers mowing lawns and pot walloping at the Dedham Golf and Polo Country Club, my savings wouldn't cover private school tuition. Lucky for me, Tilton Academy had some athletic and work scholarships. Those, combined with my savings and a little financial help from my folks, were enough to allow me to head for New Hampshire in the fall.

It was a wonderful year for me. I studied hard, got very good grades, and played three sports for the school. I also learned a number of very important lessons. As I mentioned earlier, writing was for me a fun thing to do.

One of my first compositions for my English teacher was an imaginative story, which led the reader to believe that the writer was in the military being attacked by aircraft until the last two lines disclosed the harrowing winged fighters were mosquitoes.

I thought it was pretty good and so did the teacher who called me in. He thought it was too good and implied I had plagiarized or copied the story written by an author who was much more competent than I could possibly be. I professed my innocence and was excused with a threatening, "We'll see!" Three months later after passing in many papers, I got a grudging apology from the teacher. Although I always lost points for grammar and syntax, I could put words on the paper that would in one way or another touch the reader.

One of the most important lessons of my life happened in the last month of my year at Tilton Academy. I was the captain of the tennis team, and we were enjoying a fine season. The school tennis courts were on the other side of town—a mile or so from the Academy. Late in May, on a blistering hot day, we finished our last practice before our final match of the season, which was scheduled for the next day.

Slowly, two teammates (who looked like Mutt and Jeff) and I shuffled our way back to the campus. My friends decided to stop at a package store on the route and buy beer. We were all 18 or 19—underage. I declined and waited outside the store, but they bought one for me anyway. I had two thoughts. If I drank the beer I would be breaking school and state regulations. I also knew I was very thirsty. The beer tasted wonderful.

The next day we had our last tennis match. I learned after supper that two members of the tennis team had been summoned to Dean Jeffries' office: namely, my teammates who had bought the beer the day before. I heard the package store owner or someone inside had reported the two students. Their description left no doubt. My friends were immediately suspended for two of the final three weeks of school and left for home immediately. I didn't even get the chance to speak with them.

That night I did a lot of thinking. I knew the rules of the school. In fact, as a Proctor, it had been part of my responsibility to make sure the 7th and 8th graders in my dorm understood and observed the regulations each student had agreed to before being accepted by Tilton. I didn't sleep much that night. I rationalized that it was "no big deal—one lousy beer." My parents' words would chase my excuses away. "If you make a mistake, break the accepted rules, be prepared to pay the penalty or you will spend much of your life looking over your shoulder. You know right from wrong!"

Ten A.M. the next morning, I knocked on Dean Jeffries' office door. As usual, he welcomed me cordially and asked me to sit down.

He wasn't looking for me. They were not looking for a third boy. I told him my involvement with my teammates, Slim and Stony, and he listened without a word. When I stopped, he sat in silence for a few moments. "Well, Dick," he began, "the beer you drank will be, I am sure, the most expensive beer you will ever drink in your life. In fact, it might be the most expensive beer ever drunk.

You have had a great year here at Tilton. You played three varsity sports, edited the newspaper, did an excellent job as a proctor, sang in the glee club, and earned an A- average. Graduation is three weeks away. On that day you were to have received three thousand dollars in scholarship money for your first year at Drew University where you have been accepted. I am sorry, but this morning you lost those scholarships, and you are suspended for two weeks. You may not think so now, but you made the right decision coming here."

I didn't say a word, and I certainly didn't believe his final sentence. I returned to my dorm to pack. I cried. What was I going to tell my folks who had worked so hard to give me what they could to make this year possible? It was the toughest phone call of my life. I told them I had been suspended and I was coming home for two weeks. On the phone they didn't yell—they told me they loved me, and at the time that seemed to make it even worse.

With all scholarship money gone, continuing my education was in doubt. I returned to Tilton for the final week of the year and graduation. My roommate's dad was a tanker captain for Socony Oil (later Mobil). When he learned of my plight, he kindly arranged for me to work on oil tankers for the summer; a good job for a young man needing to earn serious money. Often while in port, I was able to stand extra watches for seamen who wanted more shore time, and they paid me well. By the end of the summer, I had enough saved for my first year's tuition at Drew and a little extra. I would need to work during the school year—but I could make it. I knew that I could return to Socony the following year, so at least two years of college would be possible.

I never will forget the two summers I spent at sea. During the day, we would chip and paint, chip and paint, scrub and clean, and in port sometimes I would go down into the depths of the oil tanks to clean out the flakes of iron, the result of corrosion. That particular job paid extra as it was considered hazardous. What I really remember most was standing watch at night as a lookout.

During those solitary hours I saw, felt, and thought of so many things. The gentle, warm breeze off the Gulf of Mexico ruffled my hair, and caressed my face. A crystal clear sky allowed me to see brilliant stars as never before. The ship's bow cut through a sea of dark glass and in the wake, phosphorescent life danced and played unendingly. Often dolphins were only a few yards below me and put on a show, diving and jumping in the froth. Those nights under the stars were magical. I was at peace with myself and the world.

Only once in a while would memories take me back to my three thousand-dollar-beer and my subsequent suspension. Grudgingly, I came to the conclusion that Dean Jeffries had been right. *We make mistakes. We pay for them. We can live with ourselves. We go on with our lives.* I had learned a good lesson. One I would never forget. In the long run, doing the right thing, I felt was probably the easiest road to travel. I could face myself in the mirror and had been given a chance to earn enough money to go to college, and as a bonus, I had discovered a new-world—the world of the sea—a world I came to dearly love.

My first two years at Drew University were great fun. If you interpret this sentence to mean I didn't do much studying, you grasped the gold ring. As vice-president of a practical jokers club, our innocent but unappreciated pranks kept the school's administration looking for culprits. Miscreants replaced a container of milk with a keg of beer in the dining hall. They opened up caterpillar tent nests in the graduate seminary school's sacrosanct lounge, and launched a large, red rooster through a 3rd floor window to join the students and faculty in the dining rectory below. These were a few of our dastardly deeds but as my dad once said, "Dick, if you can't be good—be lucky!" We were. We were never caught. However, besides being a small gremlin in the smooth running machinery of the University, I did study some, managed to play three sports, dated, and worked every day to pay for my tuition.

At Drew, I met other young people from all over the world of every race, and religious persuasion. My so-so grades reflected my lifestyle. If the purpose of college had been to verbally solve the world's problems, to discuss and debate religious dogma and philosophy, then I would have earned straight A's. Along with other idealistic young people, I often stayed up until dawn verbally creating a perfect planet. The more I read, heard in the classroom and in our lounge, the more my religious beliefs became lost in the woods of cosmological literature. More than ever, I questioned the theological tenets of all religions. It was obvious to me that everyone in the world who claimed religious enlightenment could not be right. With the inability of youth to shelter conundrums under a single philosophical umbrella, I deduced that conflicting views regarding the Creator proved that in reality there isn't a knowable answer. Everyone is wrong. The Creator was "none of the above."

This mental trashing of religions was bolstered by my history courses that described the role religions have played during man's short time on this planet. Whether reading of ancient or modern times, primitive or complex societies, Eastern or Western theologies, a large number of the high priests and their devotees fostered everything from simple prejudice to genocide in the name of their religion. I wanted nothing to do with philosophies, which rationalized atrocities in the name of God or gods.

Since the day I had opened my first book, I had become a voracious and eclectic reader. In college, I was no different. One of my favorite genres was science fiction, and my favorite sci-fi author was Arthur C. Clarke. He has been called the "greatest science fiction writer of all time." In his book *2001 THE FINAL ODYSSEY*, one of his comments referring to our planet was, "Civilization and Religion are incompatible." As I continued to read and ponder world history, I sadly came to agree with Dr. Clarke.

By my 20th birthday, I was a card carrying agnostic. How could any creator whose miracles filled our world not endow the human species with the wisdom to peaceably share His gifts and also at the same time tolerate the tragic suffering of millions.

Yet, I continued to love life, people, and our beautiful world. The words of Emerson tempered my cynicism and kept meaning and purpose in my life.

> *To laugh often and much,*
> *to win respect of intelligent people*
> *and the affection of children,*
> *to earn the appreciation of honest critics*
> *and endure the betrayal of false friends,*
> *to appreciate beauty,*
> *to find the best in others,*
> *to leave the world a bit better,*
> *whether by a healthy child, a garden patch . . .*
> *to know even one life has breathed easier*
> *because you have lived.*
> *This is to have succeeded.*

"Enough!" I said to myself. I knew the world wouldn't change because I reviewed its ills until the wee hours of the morning. I wasn't getting my money's worth out of college, so in 1957 I joined the army. Looking back, that decision does not seem as logical as it did then.

After basic training I was sent to a helicopter outfit in Italy to keep the squadron's records. I decided on my second night that my first visit across the big pond was going to be more than spending free-time spit-shining shoes and drinking beer. I wanted to get to know our hosts, their culture, and their philosophies. I didn't speak Italian.

Wandering down one of the narrow streets of Vicenza I saw a sign which said *Ophanatrophio St. Dominico*. I entered the gate and a few minutes later stood before a confused priest. I wondered if I could communicate, rapidly thumbing through an English-Italian dictionary, mispronouncing every word, and still get the idea across that I would like to volunteer my time to help in any way possible. After patiently listening to my gibberish, the frustrated director spoke, "Parlez vous francais?"

My mind flashed back to my long-suffering high school French teachers who daily listened in agony to what they believed was my intentional massacre of the beautiful language. Often my pronunciation and sentence structure brought great joy to my equally inept colleagues and tears to the eyes of my French teacher. Could I remember enough French words that had been drummed into my head by my tortured teachers to convey my desire? Very slowly, I painstakingly pulled "mots" from my memory, hoping the director could fathom my wishes. I believed he nodded appropriately, so I showed up again the following night.

Every night at 5:00 P.M. I would don my civvies and rush out the base's front gate to work with the priests and kids. I taught the youngsters some English and they taught me Italian and much more. The orphans had so little. I didn't see a decent pair of shoes among the sixty plus children. They had no work, play, or dress shoes. They had only the shoes they wore every day. At the end of my first week working at the orphanage I wrote my folks about the boys of St. Dominico.

Could they possibly ask our friends in Needham, tell the people at church, relate my request to the *Needham Times,* and talk with anyone who would listen? We needed shoes and anything else that boys five to sixteen could use. Six weeks later cartons of shoes and clothes arrived at the base. My commander allowed me to load up a truck to deliver the gifts from my parents and many Needhamites. Magically, each youngster found at least one pair of shoes that fit and there were lots of extras that would eventually be adopted by needy feet.

The kids, priests, and nuns not only taught me Italian but many of life's lessons. I can't remember them all but appreciation for each day was one, food on a plate another, and caring for each other was a third. Often on weekends, I would accompany the orphanage's small band high into the mountains to bring music to poor, isolated villages that were celebrating a religious holiday.

At the orphanage, everything was shared including their faith in a loving God. There was no special menu for the adults. We all ate together. The priests, nuns, and youngsters could easily have asked God why they had been forsaken, but I don't think it ever crossed their minds. Although I remained a non-believer regarding religions, my belief in the oneness and basic goodness of man had been strengthened.

I returned home from Italy and the military more mature. Underline the word more! I had a long way to go. My experiences had shown me that true compassion and love for our fellow man does exist. I certainly was less cynical regarding the motives of human beings. In addition, to paraphrase Samuel Clemens, I was amazed at how much my parents had learned in the short time I had been away! I entered Boston University to complete my degree so that someday I could try teaching. I had a goal!

D'Ann

$\mathcal{C}hapter$ III

————•◦•————

I returned to civilian life. Daily, I drove a Volkswagen bus for the private school, Browne and Nichols, picking up eight of their students and dropping them off before proceeding to Boston University for my classes. Late in the afternoon, I would reverse my steps.

On Fridays, I would pick up my weekly pay. D'Ann O'Brien was one of the headmaster's secretaries. Miss O'Brien was twenty-five, petite, attractive, and had a wonderful smile which she bestowed on me each week. She also gave me my paycheck. How could I not fall in love with her? Three months later, I asked her if she would like to go on a camping trip to Alaska—"our honeymoon!" Although she had never pitched a tent, she agreed and a week later she was wearing a small diamond. May 26, 1962 was only a few months away.

Two weeks after becoming man and wife, we stuffed our V.W. Beetle, "sans" back seat, with camping gear. In preparing for our odyssey, we had only two disagreements. I lost both. I thought all we would need was a pup tent, but the faculty at Browne and Nichols knew better and gave us a tent that would allow us to dress standing up. I learned this is a very important tent attribute for a woman. The second bone of contention was the number of pairs of shoes D'Ann would need for the trip. I took them out of our V.W. Beetle almost as fast as she packed them. Finally, tired of being a retriever, I gave up.

Our ten-week journey was a never-to-be-forgotten kaleidoscope of experiences, which ranged from the ridiculous to the sublime. Our first "wilderness" campsite was in Ohio. After paying the admission fee, and quarreling about the correct way to put up the tent, we soon learned that behind the trees, which enclosed the campground fifty yards from our campsite, were railroad tracks. It must have been the main line to everywhere, as iron horses rumbled through hourly shaking the earth, eliminating the possibility of sleep, and raising the question, "Was this any way to start a marriage?"

A few days later, we laughed at our memory of our first night under the stars, our heated debate, and our tears shed over the mini-earthquakes created by the Cannonball Express brotherhood.

Further west magnificent vistas became life long memories. We stood in awe looking at the wonders of our national parks. The beauty of green fringed, blue serpentine rivers, nature sculptured rock formations, snow capped majestic mountains, and an abundance of birds and animals filled our days. We watched salmon fight upstream against great odds to spawn and then die. In Alaska, we kept a respectful distance from huge grizzlies that we saw feasting on the carcasses of caribou. In addition, elk, moose, fox, and golden marmots kept us loading rolls of film into our cameras.

Of course, after making camp each night, we met strangers— some became lifelong friends. Our 1500-mile dusty journey on the Alcan Highway, bordered by wilderness, shared with animals and kindred spirits, provided experiences and stories which we remembered often during our lifetime together.

In one remote site tenting by ourselves, we read in the campsite's log that grizzlies were prevalent in the area. That night D'Ann heard a prowling bear outside our tent. Chivalrously, I gave D'Ann my fishing knife so she could slash the rear of the tent and escape while Daniel Boone confronted the beast. With a hatchet in a shaking hand, I slowly pulled back the tent flap. Not two feet away, practically eyeball to eyeball, was the largest snowshoe hare I had ever seen. D'Ann and I never forgot that night and we often laughed over Alaska's bears that go hippity-hop.

Our daily-shared experiences strengthened the foundation we were building for a good marriage. In Danali National Park, the weaker sex got sick, so D'Ann became nurse, driver, cook, etc., until finally it was necessary for me to seek medical care. We were forced to sell our car, ship our belongings home, and fly back to Boston. I would convalesce in a hospital for several weeks. Macho man was gone forever.

D'Ann and I found a small apartment in Malden not far from her parents who I came to love as much as I did mine. Charles and Nina, I found, were simply wonderful people who became a welcomed integral part of our lives. I returned to teaching. Radcliff College hired D'Ann and the first of three cats became family. Our years together flew by with work, travel, and staying close to our families. D'Ann learned early in our marriage that it would never be dull, as I was a born risk-taker.

My father loved horse racing, but by taking me to the races he proved that you can beat a horse race, but you can't beat the horses. "Dick," he would often advise me, "if you want to gamble in life, gamble on yourself. Nobody wants you to succeed as much as you do."

When I first proposed a new venture, D'Ann might roll her eyes, shake her head, state her case, and even shed some tears, but eventually she would smile as if her little boy's new idea might fade away. When I committed us to a new challenge, D'Ann would jump into every endeavor with both feet.

After four years teaching and coaching at a remedial school, I decided to found a school for older boys with reading and learning problems but with average or above intelligence—youngsters who had known academic failure but had not experienced the meaning of the word success. It would take all of the five thousand dollars D'Ann and I had saved during our first four years of marriage. When we signed the lease for a building, Charles River Academy did not have one student and we were in considerable debt.

We opened in the fall of 1965 with 28 students, and by the end of the year we were at our capacity with 75 students. Our philosophy was very simple. It is unimportant what you can't do—only what you can do counts. We stressed that every individual has talents as well as disabilities and our goal was to find those talents. We emphasized athletics, art, wilderness programs, mechanical and manual professions, as well as academics, in order that each student would learn that he was a capable human being and would be able to meet the challenges of adult life. Five years later, we left Charles River Academy with a solid reputation for helping young people. We left a school with zero debt and we had operated in the black each year.

We moved to Cape Cod in 1970. D'Ann began working for Bob Chase's Insurance Agency in Harwich. Bob, his wife Jane, and family, became dear friends. I was hired as the first Dean of Students at Dennis-Yarmouth High School. Later, I served as the first educational director at the Barnstable House of Correction and then as a psychologist for the Department of Youth Services.

In 1972, we were given the opportunity to participate in Cape Cod's building boom. While working at the House of Correction, I had helped a young man earn a high school diploma. Arthur's grandfather was the captain of a sport fishing boat. The owner of the boat was the president of a bank. He called me one day thanking me for the work I had done with Arthur and asked me to meet with him. At lunch at the Harvard Club, Bill Sawyer said if D'Ann and I put all our savings, $20,000, into a building project, his bank would finance the rest. D'Ann and I talked a long time about investing our ten years of savings, our nest egg, to leverage the building of twenty-four 1500 square foot duplexes. We (I guess mostly me), decided to gamble. Upon completion, the units were quickly rented for $225.00 a month, which covered our large mortgage and taxes. D'Ann and I thought we had created a $1,000,000 long-term investment.

In 1974, the Arab countries turned off the oil flow to the U.S. and recession came to Cape Cod. Our tenants lost their jobs and couldn't pay their rent. We couldn't pay our mortgage. We lost everything but our home.

Fortunately, D'Ann had kept her job with the Chase Insurance Agency while we built our duplexes. I was hired by the Harwich School System to create a Career Education Program. For several years our goal was to get back on our feet financially but then I got another itch. One night at supper, I asked D'Ann what she thought of a backpacking trip to South America during my summer vacation. D'Ann had a way with words. She replied, "No way, Jose,— but you can go!"

Before I departed, D'Ann pinned a note on the lapel of my jacket which said, "If this man appears lost, please return him to his wife, D'Ann Wainwright, Dennis, Massachusetts, U.S.A."

Two months later I returned, having seen a different world: a world of fine artisans and gentle people, who tolerated and gently corrected my error-filled Spanish. Excitedly I showed D'Ann some of the items I had brought back and in the same breath told her we should start an import business. Her eyeballs and eyebrows went up in unison. I showed her beautiful handmade dough ornaments, told her what I paid for them, and what I thought they would sell for in the United States. She was impressed but quickly pointed out that unless I could sell each ornament for fifty dollars a piece, then we would still lose money on the trip considering the cost of the flight, food, housing, etc. I reluctantly agreed, bringing a knowing smile to D'Ann's face, but she realized I probably wouldn't let go of the idea that easily.

Some months later I told her I wanted to return to Ecuador to purchase at least two thousand ornaments along with other handmade crafts. We would wholesale them along with selling them at craft shows until we could afford a store in Dennis. D'Ann affectionately looked at her husband and gave me that "here we go again" smile.

During our twenty years of importing goods from Ecuador, Peru, Bolivia, Chile, and Bali, I made over thirty overseas trips, mostly to Ecuador. D'Ann made three with me and also came to love our Ecuadorian friends. Later my mother, Bee, mother-in-law, Nina, and staff from our store, Andean World, joined me on buying trips. D'Ann and I became very close with several families and became godparents to eight children—five have lived with us in the U.S. from one to ten years. Paquita was the first "godchild" to arrive.

She and D'Ann became "muy simpatico". I taught Paquita to drive. She taught me a lot about young ladies, patience, and prayer. Paquita returned to Ecuador after a year with us, proud of the fact that she was the only female of five in her family that could drive a car. Paquita started her own hair salon, married, and last year had her first baby.

Fredy was our second godchild to join us on the Cape. He graduated from Dennis-Yarmouth High School and went on to earn a degree from the University of Massachusetts in mechanical engineering. Pablo and Cesar came later and also graduated from D-Y then attended Cape Cod Community College.

D'Ann and I felt blessed to be part of the lives of these young people and their families. We planned to have the youngest of our Ecuadorian godchildren, Maria Augusta, come to the United States in the fall of 1995 to begin her high school career. Our close relationship with our Ecuadorian friends and their children contributed greatly to the love and joy in our life.

Still teaching, I borrowed some money so a fellow educator and I could patent an invention—namely, the Safety Bear Bathtub Spout Safety Cover. After finding an incredulous manufacturer in Illinois, our basement became our warehouse. D'Ann and I began putting Safety Bears in point of purchase boxes for stores. Marketing was a slow process as we all continued to work at full time jobs.

As more and more small stores began to order Safety Bears, a retired friend said he had nothing to do and would be happy to pack our invention. John Morrissey was a big help. After lots of sales trips, letters, demonstrations, etc., Eureka!!! We were finally discovered by a few big companies: Proctor and Gamble, Toys-R-Us, and Lillian Vernon.

I decided to take another risk and leave education and devote full time to Wainwright Enterprises Ltd./DBA Family Life Products, vis-a-vis, Safety Bear and Andean World. D'Ann's faith in me made this big jump possible.

Like all businesses, my two endeavors required a lot of hours, but over the years provided D'Ann and myself with a good living. We were able to take family vacations, travel a bit, and educate the godchildren who lived with us. Eventually D'Ann was able to semi-retire to a part time summer job in the late 1980's.

Writing

$\mathcal{C}h\ a\ p\ t\ e\ r$ IV

As a child I was a voracious reader, enjoyed writing, and listening to radio. Sunday night was the best night with the likes of Edgar Bergen and Charley McCarthy, Jack Benny, Inner Sanctum, and so many more great programs. In school, reading and writing ran a close second to sports and girls. For many years, ideas for a story simmered in my mind. It focused on a tiny Christmas tree.

When I was small my father had relatives who owned a dairy farm in St. Johnsbury, Vermont. We visited the farm for the first time late one fall. Several memories became indelible. First, being roused out of bed before the sun even thought of rising; second, stepping out into a frosty graying light and seeing my breath turn to vapor; and third, trudging to the outhouse. A booming but friendly sounding voice pierced the dawn. "Hurry up—our cows are waiting to be milked." I certainly hurried. In the cold barn it took me forever to learn enough to get an inch of milk in the pail. Ignominiously, I had to give up my stool and let a "man" finish Bossy. In addition to cows, Dad's relatives had acres of woods to explore. There I found all sizes and shapes of Christmas trees and one went home with us.

I also remembered a double pneumonia Christmas I had spent in the Newton-Wellesley hospital. My folks brought in a tiny, live, Christmas tree for my bedside table. They had decorated it with miniature ornaments and the tiny tree went home with me in February and a seed had been planted.

Throughout my life, when in the mood, I would often sit down and put words to paper. It took a while but finally in my late thirties,

I had finished the first draft of *A TINY MIRACLE*. The basic philosophy of the story was with faith, hope, and perseverance, no matter where we are born, how difficult our circumstances, or how daunting life's challenges, there is a place for each one of us in this world. Of course, D'Ann and my mother said they liked the book but their kind words did not do much for my confidence. I went further out on the limb and even asked several non-relatives. Surprise! They liked it too. Yet positive reviews from family and friends, rather than bolstering my confidence, for some reason seemed to deplete it along with my belief in any personal literary ability. I decided to do the sensible thing. I deposited the manuscript in the bottom drawer of our desk and forgot about it.

Life has a way of giving us a kick in the pants—maybe sometimes to get us to finish an important task. In 1984, I returned from a trip to Ecuador and a few days later felt rather ill. According to D'Ann my greenish-yellow complexion clashed with all our furniture and house decor. She felt we should either go to the hospital or call in an imaginative decorator. We left for the hospital where it was quickly determined I had a severe case of Non-A/Non-B Hepatitis. I was immediately pin-cushioned with needles and attached to plastic tubing. Wandering in and out of lucidity and consciousness, I realized I was one sick puppy.

How sick? I wasn't sure until my doctor called in my attorney, my best friend, and D'Ann. It seemed my bile duct was amongst the missing, and the numbers coming out of my liver were off the charts. There really was no treatment. I floated in and out of consciousness. According to my doctor, since my bile duct was probably destroyed, I probably would not survive more than sixty days; but he would ship me to Boston anyway. I heard everything. Funny, for some reason I wasn't really scared of dying but simply felt resigned and sad that my life was soon to end. I had many thoughts: D'Ann and our wonderful life together, the many people I would miss, and things that I would leave undone. I would never get to visit New Zealand—a special dream, and in my heart, I knew I should have at least tried to publish *A TINY MIRACLE*.

In Boston, friends brought in macrobiotic food, mainly soup, that I ate when I could, but mostly I just slept. While I was sleeping an amazing thing happened. The bad numbers being created by my liver stopped going higher and slowly started down toward normal. My liver shrank in size. Finally, an ecstatic doctor came in with the good news—they had found my bile duct. Where it had been I hadn't the faintest idea. The way he phrased it, I thought my bile duct must have been on a vacation in Vegas or someplace. I chuckled to myself thinking my bile duct must have lost its stake and had to return home.

The doctor's final comment was that after a year's bed rest I would be fine. I had received a wake-up call. With Nina, my wonderful mother-in-law and former nurse caring for me, I began the journey back to good health. Immediately, I began spending a few hours a day editing *A TINY MIRACLE*. I called my friend Jack Crompton, a former student of mine. He had gone to art school, married Joanne, another student of mine, and then had two boys and a girl. I asked Jack and Joanne to please read *A TINY MIRACLE* to their children and tell me what they honestly thought. They loved it. I asked Jack if he would work with me to illustrate the book.

Jack replied, "Sorry, I couldn't do that—I've never illustrated a book."

"Well, Jack," I countered, "I've never written one—we will do it together!"

Jack came to my bedside the next day. I doodled and Jack sketched. Eventually, he magically transformed my stick figures into beautiful illustrations. I continued to fine-tune the story. Almost two years passed before all the illustrations were done, and I felt that the story was as good as I could make it.

It was again time to share my hopes and new dreams with D'Ann. We went out to dinner. I told her I would like to publish *A TINY MIRACLE* and have five thousand copies printed. Including what I owed Jack for the illustrations, we would have to borrow thousands of dollars. There were no tears—only a gentle, smile. D'Ann had long ago come to believe in my dreams.

With an impish gleam in her eye, she put on a straight face and asked me who I thought would buy the books?

With an equal poker face, I told D'Ann my mother had promised to buy one, as did her mother so we had only to worry about four thousand nine hundred and ninety-eight. We both laughed.

A TINY MIRACLE was published in 1986 but we did not begin marketing it until the following year. D'Ann made another dream of mine come true. For my August birthday, she wrapped up a present with a note. It simply said, "I'll miss you, but go to New Zealand and don't worry." And I did. I spent two fantastic months backpacking, rebuilding my strength and stamina from my bout with hepatitis. I called D'Ann every Friday learning that Cape Cod had been hit again by the white stuff. The peninsula was having a terrible winter. D'Ann delighted in hearing all my exciting news as I related the joy of trekking in New Zealand's Alps, making lots of new friends, and even shearing sheep. It was summer in New Zealand and the weather was warm and sunny. D'Ann never complained that she was home alone battling the worst winter in a hundred years on Cape Cod. I realized again how lucky I had been to marry such an amazing and loving woman.

When I returned from New Zealand, I jumped into marketing *A TINY MIRACLE*.

Weekends I would set up a tent at craft shows across the state to sell and sign the book. During the week I would visit Cape Cod stores asking them to read the book, telling them if they liked it I would sell them one or more signed copies. I scheduled speaking presentations at schools, civic organizations, and churches. D'Ann would often be at my side when she wasn't home taking care of our godchildren, our house, or preparing meals.

A little more than six months after its publication, the first edition of *A TINY MIRACLE* was sold out. I began writing *POOFIN*. My goal remained to write stories for people of all ages—books that would be understood and enjoyed by young and old alike but touch adults at a much deeper level. Children would comprehend the values, the human strengths, weaknesses, and concepts, but their aunts, uncles, parents, or grandparents would relate to the stories because of personal experiences that had shaped and tested their philosophies of life.

POOFIN focused on the concept of "good intentions, the spirit of Christmas, and tears of joy." One of the reviewers wrote, "Now three year olds can understand the mystical idea of 'tears of joy' as parents often shed tears while reading your books."

Fortunately, *POOFIN* was as equally well received as *A TINY MIRACLE*. Over the next ten years, I wrote five additional books about various facets of human life.

As my stories traveled across the country, readers wrote suggesting different topics for me to consider—including death. They said a book on this subject was needed as there were few for young people that dealt with this subject.

At first I simply thanked them for their confidence in my ability but replied that it was too difficult a subject for me to tackle. All my stories have a happy ending whether they deal with courage, failure, frustrations, disabilities, prejudice, talents, tolerance, etc. I wondered how could any story about death bring comfort and peace, never mind happiness. For many years, I simply dismissed this idea as being beyond my capabilities.

In 1992, although D'Ann and I were in good health, I began picking up philosophical and spiritual books to read. Slowly, my thinking regarding death began to change as I realized the story could revolve around a celebration of life and a cosmological view I felt comfortable with—namely, the general philosophy of life of native Americans.

The sad, yet inspirational history of the American Indians and biographies of many of their famous leaders had always been an interest of mine. As I delved deeper into the Indian way of life and did research, the concept for a book on death slowly came together. Eventually the book would be entitled *NANA, GRAMPA AND TECUMSEH*. The general Indian philosophy and theology of life are that each organism: plant, animal, or human being, is intertwined with all living things during the cycle of its life. Upon completion of the cycle, the soul or energy continues in another dimension. As Chief Seattle (1786-1866) wrote, "There is no death, only a change in worlds." I felt that I could write a book on death based on this philosophy. The words of an unknown Native American poet beautifully expressed these spiritual concepts.

> *" If we look at the path,*
> *we do not see the sky.*
> *We are earth people*
> *on a spiritual journey*
> *to the stars.*
> *Our quest, our earth walk*
> *Is to look within,*
> *to know who we are,*
> *to see that we are connected*
> *to all things,*
> *that there is no separation,*
> *only in the mind. "*

Early 1995, I completed the first draft of *NANA, GRAMPA AND TECUMSEH*. As always, I began the next step in my writing process by asking friends, teachers, and librarians to read my manuscript and tell me what they did and didn't like about the story. "How can I make it better?" I would always ask.

By that time, D'Ann and I were spending part of each winter in Florida. We had purchased a small home in Palm Coast, which is 30 miles south of St. Augustine. There I would spend time writing, doing a few signings, and spending more time with D'Ann. We loved our little retreat from the snow; we walked, biked, and made many new friends. We were delighted when our northern friends would leave the cold behind and come and visit us.

When I spoke of my mother-in-law I often told people that I had been extremely lucky to get two wonderful women for the price of one. Nina, D'Ann's ninety-year old, very spry and sharp mother continued to be a big part of our life and would spend the winters with us in Florida. It was a very special time for us as we could relax, not worry about deadlines, and enjoy our semi-retirement.

We always returned to Cape Cod by May. I had a full summer and fall schedule of book signings and speaking engagements at schools. D'Ann looked forward to assisting the director of the Yachtsman Condominiums in Hyannis. Our spare time would be spent planting our flower garden, grooming our yard, and hosting friends we could entice to the Cape. We set aside Thursday evenings for summer theater at the Cape Playhouse with our friends the McGourtys. We were also looking forward to the arrival of one of our Ecuadorian godchildren, Maria Augusta, who would be joining us in the fall to begin her studies at Dennis-Yarmouth High School. We expected 1995 to be an especially happy, busy, and beautiful year on Cape Cod—we were so wrong.

Why, God?

$\mathcal{C}$ h a p t e r V

Early August 1995, D'Ann seemed to be a strong, healthy woman. She never liked to visit doctors. D'Ann believed that colds, aches, and pains were only temporary and if ignored would soon go away. Her rare trips to hospitals were to visit me. Late one night in August, D'Ann began to complain of a pain in her back. Tylenol and Motrin couldn't stop the pain and it rapidly got worse. At midnight, we took the first of three trips that night to the emergency ward of the Cape Cod Hospital. The treatment she received helped for only a few hours, and finally around 6:00 A.M., she was given a strong painkiller and admitted for extensive testing.

Late in the day, I returned to the hospital and met our family doctor and old friend, Bob Dolan. He told me D'Ann had uterine cancer. I quizzed him on the prognosis and the chances for a full recovery. He was reluctant to tell me but I was not going to leave without answers. Finally, with his hand on my shoulder, he said D'Ann's cancer had spread and any therapy would only be palliative treatment. He believed D'Ann would live about four months.

At first, I simply stared into his eyes, comprehending but refusing to believe his words. Barely I heard his words. "I'm so sorry, so sorry!"

As tears blinded me, I turned, and fled toward the exit door holding back a scream. I staggered outside, and wrapped myself around a column, yelling and cursing God. "GOD, NO, NO, NO!" My cries must have been heard in downtown Hyannis. Today, I realize the anguish I experienced is felt by thousands of people around the world, each waking hour. During those moments each one of us will never be more alone.

In a trance, I drove home. D'Ann remained in the hospital in preparation for a trip to Boston and surgery. I couldn't accept Dr. Dolan's prognosis. He had to be wrong. I began to build a denial wall. Up to two days ago, D'Ann was fine. Last night she had back pain, now she was heading for Brigham and Women's Hospital. It was too fast. Cancer would create other symptoms. Bob couldn't be right.

The chief oncologist and gynecologist at Brigham and Women's operated on D'Ann. Following the surgery, I met him. They had removed a large tumor, but he assured me that he had gotten all the cancer and D'Ann would be back for her five-year check up. I hugged him as I cried.

In a little more than forty-eight hours, I had gone from the depths of despair to singing alleluias, thanking God The Creator, praising the medical community, and reinserting our dreams for the future in my mental data bank.

When I picked Dee up, she looked great. The next night she was able to go to the theater to see the last play of the season at the Dennis Playhouse. She still complained of pain but Motrin seemed to control it. Radiation was planned, but first she had to recover from the surgery. Two weeks later, the day radiation was to begin, an MRI showed the cancer had spread. I had to tell D'Ann that chemotherapy was now our only option.

At that moment, the anger and betrayal I felt toward the members of the medical profession almost consumed me—D'Ann's faith in me, her courage, and gentle acceptance—saved me. She didn't shed a tear—only nodded.

After two chemo-treatments, we learned this treatment was not reducing the cancer. It simply made D'Ann vomit constantly, lose her hair, and was destroying her immune system. She was now on TPN (liquid food) which I prepared early each day and I connected to the stoma, which was the opening for the feeding tube to her stomach. A machine slowly pumped the liquid directly to her stomach. This was a twelve-hour procedure. At night I would lie, as always, next to her, listening to her breathing, waiting for her to wake, and tell me it was time for more morphine. Consuelo, our cat, was now the only joy we shared together as she would snuggle against D'Ann. As we patted our dearly loved pet our hands would touch and we would hold hands until D'Ann returned to sleep.

I began looking into alternative therapies. Our friend, Bob Chase, volunteered to drive us to Connecticut to meet with a doctor there. Unfortunately, D'Ann was not able to keep down the herbal treatment he prescribed. Continuing to search, I learned of a cancer center in Mexico that had a good reputation so we flew there early in November. D'Ann was now in a wheelchair.

The clinic, American Biologics, was wonderful. D'Ann had terrific care. The doctors stopped her vomiting within 24 hours and she was taken off almost all morphine that I had given her daily for over three months. It was replaced by a non-narcotic muscle-relaxer, which was able to control the pain. At the center I met many people who had been diagnosed with terminal cancer years previously and returned periodically for booster treatments. They gave me hope. During the first ten days of treatment, D'Ann was well enough to go outside so that I could push her wheelchair around the town. We window-shopped or we spent time in the sun on a patio overlooking the city. For three weeks I prayed for a miracle.

The two chemo-treatments two months earlier had devastated D'Ann's immune system. None of the three treatments she received at the clinic were able to reverse the cancer. In the fourth week, D'Ann appeared to lose the ability to concentrate and to hold a conversation. An MRI revealed the cancer had spread throughout her body including her brain. I met with Dr. Henriques a final time before telling D'Ann that the treatments had been completed and we were going home for Christmas to wait for them to kick in.

She looked at me with sad but knowing eyes and smiled. Her last smile—just for me. She never cried or told me she was dying. Yet, she had known for a long time. She had allowed me to believe that somehow—someway I could save her. On the plane home, the flight crew was very kind, arranging for D'Ann to have three seats so she could lie down as I sat behind her. Shortly after take off, she lapsed into a coma. I cried across the United States. Two days later, in our bed, a little after eleven o'clock in the morning on December 18th, I held D'Ann as she died.

During her last few hours, besides doing what had to be done, I thought of D'Ann's ninety-year old mother and how I was going to break the news to her. I had spoken with Nina the night we returned from Mexico, and simply told her that D'Ann was holding her own. Nina was a little forgetful at this point but she was well aware that D'Ann was very ill. I called her very early in the morning. I told Nina that D'Ann had had a peaceful night and I would call her that evening. An hour later, I was calling a hospice nurse as D'Ann began to hemorrhage. Three hours later I cradled D'Ann in my arms as she took her final breaths. Literally, seconds later, the phone rang. It was Nina. She spoke first. "D'Ann has died." And then she began to cry. I forced myself to speak as my tears continued. All I could say was "Yes Nina, she has. I will come shortly."

Bev Chipman, our good friend and my right hand in our business, had stopped by ten minutes earlier and was sitting in our living room. It took me about ten minutes before I had composed myself well enough to the point where I could leave D'Ann and speak to the hospice nurse who was waiting outside our room. She told me Bev was waiting downstairs. Crying, I gave her the news and asked her to please go and be with Nina until I got there. I would come as soon as the hospice nurse and I changed the bed, washed D'Ann, and changed her nightgown. Nina wanted to say good-bye to D'Ann. At that moment, I had a strange thought. D'Ann already had somehow said good-bye to her mother.

I look back on the four months from D'Ann's diagnosis to her death as the toughest period of my life. I remain in awe at D'Ann's courage. Physically and emotionally, I had done more than I thought I was capable of, yet mentally I constantly berated myself for not getting D'Ann to a doctor sooner, or being bright enough to find a cure. Years earlier, we had learned and forgotten that one of D'Ann's aunts had died of this cancer. There must have been clues. In hindsight, I could think of several, and at the same time I felt there must have been effective treatments out there. I just didn't find them in time. The windmills in my mind never stopped turning.

"Death is just a moment when dying ends."

MICHEL DE MONTAIGNE

Shut Down

$\mathcal{C}$ h a p t e r VI

All during our lives we compartmentalize our thoughts and emotions. No one could survive constantly being aware of the myriad of human and personal tragedies that happen around the clock. When crises and calamities occur to others, whether they be nearby or thousands of miles away, we may react by sending a card, dropping off food, donating to the Red Cross, or simply saying a prayer. Our mind protects us from constant depression by allowing us to file bad news deep in our sub-conscious and go on with our lives.

Following D'Ann's diagnosis, denial, hope, anger, fear, and despair had kept me in an emotionally precarious state. Giving the appearance of being a strong, capable caregiver that speaks only of hope and possible miracles was a fragile shell, which often broke in private. At times I felt to be on the edge of a precipice, which should I fall, would deposit me into another world, a world where individuals sit and stare, move forward and back in a rocking chair, and maybe mumble or hum. There I would sit, remembering nothing—no memories—no pain. Occasionally, I wondered if this would be my fate when and if I could no longer cope. Yet, since we can only live one moment at a time, I found myself holding D'Ann as she died. After she had passed, a segment of my mind shut down. It knew I could handle just so much. Like many in a state of shock or grief, my mind said simply focus on the practical and concentrate on the physical tasks that lay ahead.

The phone and doorbell rang constantly. Friends and loved ones were close at hand. Arrangements had to be made. I didn't want any free time. As the day for D'Ann's memorial service approached

I reviewed our life and the hundreds of people who had shared their lives with us. I thought not only of our thirty-three year partnership but also of our families, close friends, acquaintances, and even people whom we had met through newspapers, magazines, TV, or books. I began to put words to paper that I hoped would represent our philosophy of life. The memorial service was held December 28th at the Dennis Unitarian Church. It was a large gathering. D'Ann had many friends who deeply loved her.

My eulogy began...

"Dear family and good friends, as Rev. Gondolfo said, we are here to celebrate D'Ann's life as well as acknowledge our loss. D'Ann and I had a wonderful life together, shared thousands of experiences and challenges, and have been blessed by having so many good friends. All of us here today are painfully aware of the frailty of human life but we must remember the joy and strength of the human spirit.

Before I speak of my wife, D'Ann, I would like to tell you about a book that I began writing as a child. I add to it almost every day. It will never be finished. I call it my book of heroes.

In elementary school Ted Williams, Johnny Pesky, Babe Didrikson Zaharis, Jim Thorpe, and Jessie Owens were just a few of my heroes, but by the time I graduated to high school, lesser known individuals outnumbered the fore mentioned athletes. One was a paralyzed, wheelchair bound, perpetually upbeat young man who helped manage our basketball team—another a blind friend who became a wonderful teacher.

Physically and mentally challenged individuals, like my brother, Bob, an epileptic, made me take a longer and harder look at life. It was easy to realize how lucky I was. I met and became friends with young women and men who struggled to survive in unhappy homes yet remained positive toward life.

Others, who worked long hours after school, participated in civic organizations, and still were able to obtain good grades.

By the end of high school, my idea of a hero had changed tremendously, and most celebrities failed my new criteria. Ordinary people doing extraordinary things, under difficult circumstances, replaced them. Before I turned eighteen, my parents had been entered in my book of heroes.

As I entered teaching, I had the privilege of working with hundreds of heroes: students and parents. I met parents who fed, clothed, and provided their children with the values and an education that would give them the opportunity to live happy and productive lives. Even more amazing to me were the parents whose children were physically or mentally challenged, yet proclaimed how fortunate they were to have such children.

I shall never forget the dyslexic and physically challenged girls and boys at our school who climbed their personal mountains, one step at a time, to become capable, confident, and loving adults. Their faces are forever etched in my mind. And of course, we all remember the men and women who gave their lives protecting ours.

Today my book of heroes includes such names as Beethoven, Mother Theresa, John White, Shindler and Gandhi, D'Ann and you. Through the years of our friendship, D'Ann and I came to know of the trials and challenges you all have had to face and conquer and the tragedies you have had to endure. You are all heroes in my unfinished book—just as D'Ann has been for over thirty-three years.

I knew before our wedding that I was a very lucky man to have been able to persuade D'Ann to be my wife. And during those thirty-three years, my friends, mother, and mother-in-law frequently reminded me of this fact. Before we were married, I showed up for a date one evening wearing stripes and plaids. D'Ann realized she had a real project ahead. From our engagement on, D'Ann always checked my attire before I appeared in public. Before we left for treatment in Mexico, as ill as she was, D'Ann watched and approved my selection of our clothes as I packed.

D'Ann loved life and people. They loved her in return. She supported me in every endeavor, asked for little, and was willing to share whatever we had with others. She was a hard and loyal worker for her employers. She possessed an aura of contentment and happiness that captured everyone she met. D'Ann faced life and death with courage and dignity. Not once during her five month battle with cancer did I hear a "poor me" or "why me?" Even in pain she never complained. She had an internal strength I watched in wonder. I remain in awe of her indomitable spirit.

Those of us whose lives have been entwined with D'Ann's, know that she will remain with us forever. We will continue our journey together.

D'Ann, I know, wants me to thank all those friends who brought food to our home for Fredy, Cesar, Pablo, and myself, allowing us to spend more time with her. We want to thank Nina, D'Ann's mom, who did our laundry and so much more as we cared for D'Ann. And of course, my mom, Bee, who wrote us almost daily, buoying our spirits. There are so many people to thank. All who sent flowers, cards, cheery gifts or notes, and by other acts of love and concern, reminded us daily that we were not and never would be alone.

D'Ann loved our godchildren no less than if they were our own children. As I said, she loved people. Nothing pleased her more than to have people come to our home. Nothing in this world made her happier than decorating our home and preparing for guests whether there were to be four or forty. D'Ann taught by example. She thought of others first.

*In closing, I would like to share three poems with you. The first is entitled **THE BRIDGEBUILDERS**. It reflects our philosophy of life. The second is a poem D'Ann saved from her youth and which, I believe, describes her religious convictions. The third is from a German folk song that I was given by my mother, and expresses my feelings for my wife, D'Ann.*

THE BRIDGEBUILDER

BY MISS WILL ALLEN DRUMGOOLE

An old man going on a highway,
Came at evening cold and gray
To a chasm vast and deep and wide,
Through which was flowing a swollen tide.
The old man crossed in the twilight dim,
That swollen stream held no fears for him.
But he paused when safe on the other side,
And built a bridge to span the tide.

"Old man," said a fellow Pilgrim near,
"You waste your strength by building here.
Your journey will end with the ending day:
You never again will pass this way.
You have crossed this chasm deep and wide:
Why build this bridge at eventide?"

The builder lifted his old gray head,
"Good friend, in the path I've come," he said,
"There comes after me today,
a youth whose feet must pass this way.
This swollen stream, which was naught to me,
To that fair-haired youth may a pitfall be.
He, too, must cross in the twilight dim,
Good friend, I am building this bridge for him."

LIFE'S WEAVING

My life is but a weaving between my God and me.
I may not choose the colors, He knows what they should be.
For He can view the pattern upon the upper side
While I can see it only on this, the under side.

Sometimes He weaveth sorrow, which seemeth strange to me.
But I will trust His judgment and work on faithfully.
'Tis He who fills the shuttle, He knows just what is best,
So I shall weave in earnest and leave with Him the rest.

At last when life is ended, with Him I shall abide,
Then I may view the pattern upon the upper side.
Then I shall know the reason why pain and joy entwined
Was woven in the fabric of life that God designed.

HOW CAN I LEAVE THEE

How can I leave thee?
How can I from thee part,
Thou only hast my heart,
Dear one believe.
Thou hast this soul of mine
So closely bound to thine,
No other can I love,
Save thee alone.

My dear friends and family, D'Ann and I love you very much.
You will always be in our prayers. D'Ann, I love you. You will always
be part of me and I know your spirit is with us today.
We thank each one of you for coming. God bless you."

Healing...
A Rocky, Challenging
Road

C h a p t e r VII

During D'Ann's illness, two books relating spiritual experiences were given to me. They were the first books of this nature that I had read for a long time. The first gave me hope and encouragement even as we fought a losing battle. On learning of D'Ann's ominous diagnosis, a good friend, Ken Brynildsen gave me *EMBRACED BY THE LIGHT*.

In Mexico, I had the good fortune to meet Dr. Heber Kimball. At six feet four inches he is a giant of a man yet his size is small when compared to his wisdom, compassion, and love. Heber was at the clinic because his son Jason was receiving treatment. D'Ann and I quickly came to accept him as a dear friend and he personally helped me cope during some very difficult days. Heber gave me his copy of *AUTOBIOGRAPHY OF A YOGI*. It is the story of Paramahansa Yogananda who came to the U.S. in 1935. He founded the Self-Realization Fellowship, which is now worldwide. His book has been translated into 16 languages and used as a text at over 100 colleges and universities. These two books led to many others.

During D'Ann's illness, Nina's physical and mental health suffered dramatically. Her weight dropped to eighty-seven pounds and her short-term memory loss and confusion grew. In four months, an amazingly active and spry ninety-year old became very frail. By the time D'Ann died, Nina was not able to adequately care for herself. She had no living relatives except me. D'Ann knew I loved Nina dearly. I often said that I had been extremely lucky to get two wonderful women for the price of one. I really meant it.

Early in January 1996, I took Nina to Florida to our home there. I cooked and watched over her as we began to face our loss. D'Ann had been the chef of the family, so now I had to learn to read a cookbook and follow her directions so Nina didn't have to eat just frozen dinners and spaghetti. Slowly, she began to gain weight as I insisted she eat three meals a day and drink one or more glasses of Ensure. By April, Nina was close to one hundred pounds, yet it remained a battle to get her to eat. She simply did not want to live anymore and couldn't understand why she was still living at ninety and her daughter had died at fifty-nine. When we returned to Cape Cod, our boys Fredy, Cesar, and Pablo helped me see to it that Nina continued to eat three meals a day in her own home.

By the middle of May, I was physically and emotionally at the lowest point of my life. I felt overwhelmed by the loss of D'Ann, my failure to anticipate her cancer, or find a cure, along with the responsibility of caring and making decisions for Nina. I needed to get away. I decided to spend two weeks at our time-share on Marco Island. Our boys would look after Nina.

As I drove through Rhode Island, I kept replaying the past eight months over and over again. Somewhere on Route 95, I completely lost it. I moaned and cried. Tears literally eliminated my vision. I did not know or care where I was or whether I lived or died. I totally forgot my responsibilities to other loved ones. My psychological ability to cope was gone.

My head hit the steering wheel and my foot flattened the gas pedal. Fifteen or twenty seconds went by. A siren and a flashing blue light brought me back to reality. I looked at the speedometer. I had gone from sixty to over ninety miles an hour. I slowed down and pulled over as the trooper pulled in behind me.

When he got to the window of my car, I was still crying. The officer didn't yell but in a concerned voice asked what was wrong. The dam broke. I told him everything that had happened and how I felt about life. He patiently listened. In a few minutes, I had more or less regained control. The officer first wanted to know if I thought I could safely continue such a long trip without breaking down again. I said I thought I could. He then said he had to give me a ticket but suggested I include a letter explaining what had happened. His name was Officer Smuts, badge # 70. As he suggested, I waited another five minutes before returning to the highway. Less than a quarter of a mile away, there was a long sweeping curve that would have ended my life and possibly the lives of others.

I held it together, more or less, the rest of the trip south. When I got to Marco, while looking at the ocean, I wrote the letter as Officer Smuts had suggested, mailed it with the speeding ticket and forgot about it. Two weeks later when I returned home, I called the Rhode Island state police. I wanted to at least drop the officer a note and thank him for his kindness. If he had children I planned to send him some of my books. I was told there was no Officer Smuts in the Rhode Island State Police and all badge numbers consisted of four numbers. Nine months later I received a letter from a Rhode Island judge dismissing my ticket.

While in Florida, I rested, read, and wrote the following:

FIVE MONTHS

Has she really gone?
How long before I can answer...
Yes, she has really gone.

Hours pass without tears—
Often there are sad smiles and occasionally,
Laughter with friends.

I try to live totally in the moment yet,
Slowly, I am beginning to believe those
Who assured me life will get better.

Four months ago,
I knew they were wrong.
Disbelief, despair, and anguish linger waiting—
For a remembrance of places we went and things we did,

Images of silly little gifts, our love we shared with so many, and
Our final embrace as I kissed my tears on her cheek.
Was that yesterday?
Has it really been five months since she left me.
Is the pain easing? Am I healing?
Is the gentle mist of acceptance surrounding my heart?

Will I ever again be at peace with the Creator?
Dare I risk replacing my bitterness with love?
My soul tells me, D'Ann would want and expect nothing less.
It will be hard but I will try.

MAY 18, 1996

As days went by I read a few books on grieving, along with Tom Clancy, Mary Higgins-Clark, John Grisham, Arthur Clarke, and others. I tried meditating a short time each day but found it very difficult. To sit still, empty the mind of thoughts, and concentrate on my breathing wasn't easy. It seemed impossible to chase memories, concerns, and worries which seemed to enter my mind from every direction. I did begin to pray, not sure I was praying to anyone, yet I asked for the strength I would need to take care of Nina, my family, and continue my life.

I felt that I must finish and publish **NANA, GRAMPA AND TECUMSEH**. It had taken over three years to write. Thankfully, the text was completed before D'Ann was diagnosed with cancer. It is a story, which focuses on the cycle of life for all creatures. Since it dealt with death, it was the most difficult book for me to write, considering all my books have happy endings. As I mentioned, the American Indian's philosophy of life and spirituality provided the philosophical background. I was pleased at the reaction of my proofreaders. They and I thought it was the best I had done with a very challenging theme. Later that year, Ron Walotsky, my friend and a wonderful illustrator, sat down with me, and we began sketching out the thirty-six illustrations.

I continued editing the book, reviewing the research, and re-reading histories of the way of life of native peoples. I reread of their beliefs, which I admired and had forgotten. Aborigines', including Native Americans', lives were made up of daily routines, special events, traditions, and a spiritual life, which were tightly intertwined. They believed that dying was simply a transition from one dimension to another. Often, old, infirm members of a tribe would decide when it was their time to leave this plane. After saying their good-byes to all their loved ones, they would be conveyed to a spot of their choosing. A temporary shelter would be constructed where they would remain with sufficient clothes or blankets to keep them warm and water to drink. Here, during their final days, they would remain, peacefully contemplating the beauty of the world and the joyous events of their life while looking forward to seeing loved ones again.

Today, few in the world choose this option. Why are we so afraid of death? Why can we not truly believe it is a transition for a loved one or for ourselves? When did we (humanity in general) lose a sincere belief in a spiritual after life? Although most religions list such a belief in their dogmas, I often wonder how many people in the world have no doubts that another dimension exists.

I had no, and I have no, answers to these questions. When I was faced with the loss of a loved one, I certainly reacted like most people do today—I denied it, didn't even discuss the possibility of death with D'Ann, and did everything medically possible to keep my loved one with me.

Searching

$$Chapter \text{ VIII}$$

I can remember in Sunday school teachers assuring us little tykes that all good people when they died went straight to heaven where God, a very old man with a long white beard, waited in a comfortable chair or cloud, to greet us. We would get wings and flit about a land where we could fulfill our every dream and desire. I imagined clouds dotted with ice cream cones which only melted when you licked them. Our teacher called this place heaven. It sounded like a great place to us. When I was chastised for misbehavior, I thought, "Boy! I can hardly wait to get to heaven where God will understand me."

Of course, it wasn't long before this picture of our afterlife became muddied. After learning to read, I found that Death was called the grim reaper. People who died "before their time" were considered to have died tragically. Nobody I met or read about was really looking forward to heaven. In fact, it seemed no one wanted to go. Doctors did everything possible to keep people alive as long as possible even when the quality of their lives had long passed. Dante Alighieri confused the issue by introducing me to hell where tormented souls spent eternity. By the time I graduated from high school, I realized Christianity and its followers, as a whole, were as confused as I regarding what happens, if anything, after death.

Studying other religions and their concepts of the afterlife didn't provide any definitive answers. What I wanted to read were the words of a contemporary, someone, anyone, who was believable and had returned after dying with a detailed report of life on the other side and maybe a small souvenir like a spare set of wings or personal note from my dad.

Before D'Ann's death, my reading of spiritual literature was very limited. The memories of the few serious articles and books was intermingled in my mind with movies of séances where tables moved, faces appeared in large glass fish bowls, and the charlatans were always exposed as goofy, greedy, and inept frauds. No friends or acquaintances ever told me of a paranormal experience or claimed to have psychic abilities. I had read of St. Joan of Arc and a few other notables of history who claimed to have had visions, the gift of prophesy, or the ability to communicate with spirits. At the time I considered it little more than somebody's fantasy or wishful thinking. It is easy to question and even dismiss ancient written history as being much less than factual.

Sending a message around a room, when repeated, changes quickly, proving that the spoken word is not reliable. How much truth could there be in books that were written from stories that had been passed on for generations? My position was, we simply can't know. Historical writings that describe miracles, visions, and revelations are at best inaccurate and at worst total fiction. I believed we could only communicate with the living and that if there was another dimension—a greater power—then I would have to wait until death to find out. That is what I believed when I lost D'Ann.

One of the books I read during the first year after D'Ann's death was **WE DO NOT DIE**. This was the first book written about George Anderson by Martin and Romanowski. George Anderson discovered at an early age that he was able to serve as a medium or receiver for those in the spirit world. As a youngster his ability was accepted by few and created a rather unhappy childhood. As I read the story of his life and work (George is now in his late forties), I was intrigued but remained skeptical of anyone having this ability.

Yet, my readings had led me to the point of at least considering that it might be possible. My doubts remained but I wanted to hear more and if possible meet face to face. I learned that George, for over 25 years, had done thousands of discernments over the phone, on radio, on television (*Larry King, Oprah, Roseanne, 48 Hours, Lifetime, etc.*), in large groups, small groups, and with hundreds of individuals all over the world.

The messages he relayed from those who have passed convinced the recipients that they had heard from departed loved ones.

The more I read, the more amazing it sounded. I learned George Anderson is given only the first name of the person who hopes to hear from loved ones that have passed and that person is restricted by George to answer statements with a simple Yes or No. To authenticate their presence, spiritual loved ones mention specific names or incidents that only the living would know.

I wanted to believe that such ability was truly possible and that D'Ann was fine in another dimension but I knew reading books alone would not convince me. During the three years following D'Ann's passing I occasionally read spiritual books. Nina needed more and more care. Often alone, I would weep uncontrollably as I prepared our house for sale, sorted through all our stuff, and returned to places on Cape Cod where D'Ann and I had enjoyed our life together. My memories were so vivid that tears would flow unashamedly even in the midst of a conversation when our life together was mentioned.

In Florida, one of our three bedrooms became my memory room with several large framed collages containing hundreds of photos of D'Ann and our friends in the north and south. I framed D'Ann's last Christmas card and my last card to her, I put out a few small items from our life together, and displayed one of the poems that meant a lot to us. Often in this room I would talk with D'Ann and pray for her along with all our loved ones who had died. Then I would meditate for a short period of time. I was always more at peace with life and myself after spending a little quiet time in my memory room.

Back on Cape Cod, preparing our house for sale was physically demanding but even more emotionally difficult. One of our dear friends, Lois Woodward, came down to the Cape to help me sort through D'Ann's personal items and pack them in boxes.

It was hard to decide what to keep or what to throw or give away as each item brought back a memory. Before putting the house on the market much had to be done. We needed a new title five septic system, interior painting, carpeting, and some landscaping.

Nina now required twenty-four hour care. She was suffering from severe neck and shoulder pain. One doctor thought it was spinal disks but even with strong medication it grew worse. The medication had serious side effects so we sought a second opinion. Finally a neurologist correctly diagnosed carpal tunnel syndrome. Nina had laser surgery. Like a magic bullet, after her wrists were done, Nina's pain went away, her health and stamina improved and except for her failing short-term memory, she didn't even need an aspirin.

Although Nina was feeling much better, it was time to look into an assisted living complex. Before we returned to Florida she spent a month at Thirwood Place in South Yarmouth. I was impressed with Thirwood's capable and caring staff. Everyone liked Nina and in turn she thought her apartment, the dining room, and activities were very good. We agreed that in April she would enter Thirwood, but first she would spend the winter with me in Florida.

I continued to read a wide variety of books including two other books written about the medium George Anderson, **WE ARE NOT FORGOTTEN** and **OUR CHILDREN FOREVER**. If they were to be believed then D'Ann and all loved ones are doing just fine. Everyone continues their spiritual journey after death. I wondered if I could possibly get an appointment for a discernment with George Anderson.

In the fall of 1997, through Berkley Publishing, I contacted the George Anderson Grief Foundation. I learned that Mr. Anderson sees a small number of individuals yearly. Several weeks later, I was able to schedule an appointment to meet with him the following April.

On April 9, 1998, accompanied by a friend and neighbor, Rita Horner, I left Palm Coast early in the morning for Fort Lauderdale. Nina remained in our home in the capable care of Piroska Gorog. It was a little more than a four hour drive so we had time for a late lunch before our 4:00 P.M. appointment with George Anderson at the Riverside Hotel. In the lobby, Andrew Barone, who serves as a coordinator for George Anderson, greeted us. Andrew was a very pleasant young man who readily answered our questions. "How long would the session last?" I asked.

Andrew told us, "George has no control over that. It is the spirits who wish to communicate with you that determine the length of time. It ranges from thirty minutes to one and one-half hours depending on the number of those who have passed who wish to send a message. Today, George has his maximum of six discernments and we are now about an hour behind our appointment schedule."

My second question was, "Do loved ones who have passed on always show up?" Andrew replied, "First of all, you can count on the spirits who wish to communicate with you being here. George has done thousands of discernments and never once have departed loved ones failed to communicate. It seems the spirit world is not in a distant galaxy but simply all around us—just another dimension. Your loved ones watch over you, know how you are doing, and want to send you messages."

It was quarter to five. The three previous discernments had all gone over an hour. Soon we were following Andrew to the second floor. I was nervous. In the small living room of a suite, George Anderson, in a soft voice and with a smile introduced himself.

We were told simply to give our first names. I spoke, "Hello, I'm Richard and this is Rita. Nice to meet you."

George Anderson is a small man, maybe five feet six or seven with short graying hair, a close cropped beard and a very gentle demeanor. He was dressed casually in a brown sport shirt and wore a crucifix on a chain around his neck. He reminded me that I was to respond to all his statements with yes, no, I understand, or I don't understand. I was not to give him any feedback.

Rita sat on the sofa facing George. I sat a few feet away also looking directly at him. I turned on the tape recorder we had brought and placed it on the coffee table.

George Anderson

"Although I try to stay on schedule, it seems impossible today so we're backed up good. You waited this long—what difference does an hour make?"

Richard

"Right."

George Anderson

"Well, first of all a female presence comes up behind you. Now two more. There is talk of a female that passed. Now, that could be by generation. Like you know, mother, grandmother, whatever. Let me just leave it alone. Let me say yes and assume it makes sense and also there is talk about a younger male. Yeah . . . whoever the younger male is, is clear enough to say to me, 'This is my age.' So he must've been young in understanding of age when he passed on. Without explaining, do you understand why someone is walking around and saying, 'Dad is here.' "

Richard

"YES."

(My first thought was D'Ann was speaking and was referring to her father who died many years ago but my second thought was that D'Ann usually referred to her father as "Daddy.")

George Anderson

"I'm confused. I don't know if Dad's your . . . your dad, if he has passed on . . . Several males are in the room. There's talk about . . . the loss of a son. Does that make sense? It's not yours."

Richard.

"NO."

(I was thinking only of D'Ann and not any other members of my family. I did not think of my brother who had died at age thirty-seven—eighteen years ago.)

George Anderson

"Wait a minute. No, it has to make sense. Somebody is bringing it up again. Let's leave it alone. Who ever this person is could be a son to somebody else, but not to you. Because they are saying to me, there's . . . somebody in the crowd talking about the son that passed on. And when I brought it to your attention . . . he said, 'I'm not his.' Okay, somebody said, 'Dad is here.' Is it correct your dad passed on?"

Richard

"YES."

(My dad died at age 67 on Thanksgiving Day, 1974.)

George Anderson

"Okay, so the man, who is saying, 'Dad is here' must be referring to your dad. Now he says, his father's parents have passed on."

Richard

"YES."

George Anderson

"I was going to say, unless they're two hundred years old, more than likely they have."

Richard

"YES."

George Anderson

"There is also talk about the loss of a brother. Does that make sense?"

Richard

"YES."

George Anderson

"He's the son. That's why I don't want you to explain. Let them explain. Somebody said Dad is here . . . then I heard somebody in that shuffle of people talking about the son that passed on. Then I heard the younger male say, 'I'm not his son.' And then somebody said, 'My son is with me, his brother.' Your mom's parents are passed over, yes?"

Richard

"YES."

George Anderson

"Yeah. Cause they're present. Then your brother keeps bringing up your mother but he's not telling me anything. I don't know if she is here or there. He's going to have to tell me if she's there or not. Your brother feels he could have been a little closer to you. You don't hate each other, don't get me wrong but he actually feels he could have been closer. He seems like an okay guy, but feels he could've been closer. And I think its just . . . that was the type of person he was. Oh, no, wait a minute. He says at the end . . . did he have health trouble?"

Richard

"YES."

(My brother was born with epilepsy and his continual seizures affected him emotionally and intellectually all his life. There were eleven years between Robert and me.)

George Anderson

"Cause he feels he could've been closer, so maybe you know, the health problems prevented him from being his normal self. Your brother certainly passes young by today's standards, yes? Again, wait a minute, he's saying again, 'Mom is here.' Is it correct, your mom is still on earth?"

Richard

"YES."

George Anderson

"Okay. He keeps saying. 'Mom is here. Mom is here.' Please tell Mom you've heard from him. Because your father and brother are together, which is something you might have been wondering about. I'm not trying to be funny but I keep seeing the old TV show *Leave It to Beaver.*"

Richard

"YES."

George Anderson

"And probably another reason I'm probably seeing *Leave It to Beaver* is because of the two boys, Wally and Beaver, you know the two brothers, but your father jokes at me. He wasn't exactly Ward Cleaver, but he was pretty close. Yeah, cause your father put an American flag over your head and says you had a normal American home life. Unlike me, who was raised in a neurotic Catholic yelling household, that's completely removed from you. Your brother thanks you for praying for him, so I assume you have in your own way."

Richard

"YES."

George Anderson

"Cause you and he are pals, yes? He comes to you—well, he's coming to you as a pal. Wait a second, I saw crossed lines in front of you. Is it correct your brother could have been closer to you?"

Richard

"YES."

George Anderson

"That's probably why I'm getting the cross. Even your father suggests you could have been closer. Your brother admits having a lot of struggle on earth. Is that true? More with himself?"

Richard

"YES."

George Anderson

"More with himself?"

Richard

"YES."

George Anderson

"So apparently the struggle is within. Your brother shows me a Dr. Jeckyll and Mr. Hyde. There might have been part of him you didn't know."

Richard

"YES."

(My brother was aware, at a very early age, of his illness and limited academic abilities. He was terrific fixing a bike or lawnmower but was always in a special class in school. I believe his illness destroyed his self-esteem and the ability to appreciate the talents he possessed. The fact his sisters and brother were all at least average students set him apart.)

George Anderson

"Okay. Your brother just wants you to know that he always loved you, even at times when it might not have been shown or discussed. I feel he is a very sensitive guy but didn't know how to convey his sensitivity."

Richard

"YES."

George Anderson

"I see a locked chest. I see it in front of me. He might have worn a mask. Again the book, Dr. Jerkyll and Mr. Hyde. He says he has come to you in your dreams. He keeps telling me he's all right over there. Then there must be a reason, because he says you worried about him being all right. Something to do with his passing. Your brother claims a tragic passing. Is that true?"

Richard

"YES."

George Anderson

"Age as well as circumstances? He also wants you to know you never let him down. Does that make sense?"

Richard

"YES."

George Anderson

"Yeah. He keeps saying, you never let me down and you did not fail me. Cause he feels as time went on that you became distant. Is that true? Cause you seemed closer as boys, as children. Again, that *Leave It to Beaver* relationship. But as time goes on, I'm getting this. We're going our own way and your brother puts an ice cube in front of you admitting your relationship—'might have gotten a little cool with you.' Not the other way around. 'I mean, yeah, it takes two to tango,' he says. Okay fine, cause he knows you want to accept part of it. So he says all right but he's putting more on his end. The later part of his life, your brother gives me the feeling he wasn't the happiest person. Is that true?"

Richard

"YES."

(Bob loved the phrase "it takes two to tango" and frequently used it to describe positive and negative interpersonal contact.)

George Anderson

"Well, yes, but he says, that I couldn't ask if you would agree. You don't know what he feels, you can't say yes to me. It's funny; your brother kind of challenged me. Why am I asking you, if you agree? How could you know what's inside him? You have prayed for him in your own way. He thanks you. You are not religious but you are spiritual. He also thanks you for the memorial. Does that make sense? I don't know what he means."

Richard

"NO."

(Without thinking or reflecting I answered NO because at first I thought Bob was referring to his head stone or burial. I was out of the country when he died. A split second later I realized Bob was probably referring to the dedication to him I included in my book MOUNTAINS TO CLIMB.)

"TO: Bob, my brother, who courageously battled epilepsy every day of his life."

George Anderson

"I'm going to leave it with you. He says thanks for the memorial. Unless through prayer or something you did or some memorial. That's all I can assume. He speaks of family around you. Do you have your own family? I'm confused. He's speaking of family around you. Do you have a wife and children? I mean you are not married now, you were at one time with a family. It's still a family. Also, I see professional symbols around you. Do you work in the professional area—involved with schools?"

Richard

"YES."

George Anderson

"Okay. There is also a feeling of being in control. Are you kind of self-employed?"

Richard

"YES."

George Anderson

"Okay. And I do see finance around you, so either you work with it or there is gain through your work. I mean, its not you're a multi-millionaire but you are paying your bills. Now, I don't understand and don't take me the wrong way. Your brother admits he was ready to pass on. Does this make sense?"

Richard

"YES."

George Anderson

"Your brother again speaks of a lot of struggle on earth. Is that true? But you didn't know about it?"

Richard

"NO."

(Of course, I was aware of the physical manifestations of his disease such as his seizures, memory loss, moodiness, and anger. Yet, I really never knew or realized how much his condition hurt him emotionally. As a family we never discussed it. Not a good excuse—but as a kid I was too wrapped up in my own life.)

George Anderson

"You saw him as Dr. Jerkyl and Mr. Hyde. Maybe you didn't see the torment and that is why he is saying you don't know about it. He speaks of an emotional struggle on earth. Does that make sense?"

Richard

"YES."

George Anderson

"He speaks of an emotional and health problem too, correct?"

Richard

"YES."

George Anderson

"But there's—he emphasizes there's a physical problem. Cause he says he knew he was going to pass on. Is that true? He says towards the end of his life it was very difficult for him, and his life kind of literally went down the toilet. He is chuckling! Do you understand this?"

Richard

"YES."

(At the time just before his death, my brother was having grand-mal seizures frequently which couldn't be controlled by his medication. He was admitted to the Deaconess Hospital for testing with different medications. While there one day, he went into his bathroom, sat on the toilet, and had a grand-mal seizure. His head dropped to his chest cutting off his air passage and oxygen to the lungs. When the staff found him he was clinically dead.)

George Anderson

"I mean, he might've struggled before that but when the time comes, I feel like when I go to sleep and let go. I see St. Joseph. St. Joseph is the patron saint of a happy death: your brother passes peacefully into the hereafter. When the time comes, he says he goes to sleep. Was he in some sort of a coma before he passes?"

Richard

"YES."

(Bob was in a coma for six weeks before he died of pneumonia.)

George Anderson

"I feel like, I'm—I've been asleep for a while. Like I'm in a coma. He keeps telling me he is walking fine. That means he had trouble with his legs or my symbol for his back. It affects a large part of his body."

Richard

"YES."

(Bob's balance was affected because of the hundreds of seizures he had. At times he was very unsteady on his feet.)

George Anderson

"Cause once it is diagnosed, it is pretty certain you're going to pass on? Well, that is what he states, so all right. Now he talks about it being a serious enough illness like cancer. Is that true? 'Like' is the key word."

Richard

"YES."

George Anderson

"He also has trouble breathing. Correct? When it is under control, he can live with it. But it comes on as a surprise. Apparently, the illness is treatable, yes? To a degree?"

Richard

"YES."

George Anderson

"Yeah. Like if you had cancer that's treatable, you go on chemo-therapy but that doesn't mean there's any promise with it. The thing is, he's stating, it is treatable—eventually, he says it causes him to go to sleep. Apparently it takes its toll. But yet there's the surprise factor, it catches him off guard, catches him by surprise as it is being treated, he seems to be doing all right and then bingo, it takes a turn for the worse."

Richard

"YES."

George Anderson

"That's what I call service. Cause it's funny. I just started thinking this guy has no problem giving me his name. Then I heard, Bob—Robert. Why does he keep saying he's walking and crying. Does that make sense? Did it affect his balance?"

Richard

"YES."

George Anderson

"I think the family may refer to him as Bobby. Why is there talk of another brother? Did your mom ever have a miscarriage?"

Richard

"Not to my knowledge."

George Anderson

"Well, your brother is bringing it up. If the cycle of birth had continued it would have been another boy or unless one of your parents lost a brother. Do you have contact with your mother?"

Richard

"YES."

(We did call my brother Bobby and my mother lost her youngest brother, Alfred—"Al," many years ago.)

George Anderson

"Because Bobby keeps going to your mother and saying please tell Mom you've heard from me. 'Whether she believes it or not, who cares?' He just wants her to know he's all right. Your brother seems to have a nice sense of humor. He jokes, 'whether you believe it or not, who cares, because—everybody's going to pass and find out I am right as usual, so it doesn't matter.' I think he became weary of life. There's a funny feeling in the head, like dizziness. Does that make sense?"

Richard

"YES."

(The phraseology and comment is typical of what my brother would say and how he would say it.)

George Anderson

"This I don't understand—when he says the illness is brain centered. He says it slows the heart, makes breathing difficult—he's joking with me saying, 'testing, do you read me?' So apparently, the brain's not getting the signals to the rest of the body. He does bless you for being so good to him when he was on earth. You think you could have done more for him. He puts a big hook in front of you to let yourself off the hook. Your brother shows me the cowardly lion in the Wizard of Oz, which means courage, so apparently he was fighting courageously. He never wanted to be a burden to himself or anybody else."

Richard

"YES."

(In the previous paragraph, George relays one of my brother's very frequent expressions. "Testing, do you read me?" In fact, Robert's lifelong difficulty concisely expressing himself and his tendency to ramble was in character during his communication through George.)

George Anderson

"He keeps saying, he is speaking fine and seeing fine. Does that make sense? Did this illness effect his speech and sight? Yeah. He says it's brain centered and the signals become cross-wired. I have to be honest with you I don't know what he is talking about, so I'm glad you do."

Richard

"YES, I understand."

(Bob was on medication almost all of his life. The hundreds of seizures he had during his life affected his walking, sight, and his daily emotional state.)

George Anderson

"Your brother sends his love to a Bill or a William and family. He says he spent a lot of time with them. Two other individuals want to say something. They say they are Bill's parents and they send their love but are concerned with Bill's health. Does this make sense?"

Richard

"YES."

(My brother-in-law is Bill. Bobby stayed with my sister Nancy and Bill for quite a while and lived near them for several years. Bill's health problems have gotten significantly worse during the past few years.)

George Anderson

"Your dad is a little upset, as it seems I have the impression he only had two boys. He wants to be sure I know he is sending his love to all his children. I see a picture of a tree and your dad indicates you have done a number of different things in your life and for the most part pretty well. He is proud of your latest career. I am hearing that your father's name is Ed. Is that right?"

Richard

"YES."

George Anderson

"Your brother or father is sending his love to a John and George. Do you understand?"

Richard

"NO."

(In discussing this communication with family members we recalled Bob had a friend by the name of John Mullen but we couldn't think of a George. The individual might have been a resident of the group home Bob lived in for several years.)

George Anderson

"A female by the name of Marguerite sends you love."

Richard

"YES."

(Marguerite Fardy was an aunt of my father's and was especially close to our family.)

George Anderson

"I see the color green around you, which usually indicates you are either buying or selling property. Does that make sense?"

Richard

"YES."

(At the time, I was preparing our house and my mother-in-law's house for sale.)

George Anderson

"Your brother is telling me that during the last few years there have been a lot of clouds in your life. The clouds seem to be moving away. I see a picture of covered wagons, which indicates that your life will get moving again. He also says he is your guardian angel. Your father is asking me to ask about your spouse. The female presence behind you is showing me a picture with a munchkin from the Wizard of Oz holding a sign saying, 'The End.' Did your wife die?"

Richard

"YES."

(At that point, I broke down and wept thinking finally that I would hear from D'Ann. D'Ann's first name was Dorothy, so the sign had a dual meaning.)

George Anderson

"Your wife says that neither one of you could have known she had had cancer for several years. She says it was in her private parts. The first symptom was back pain. Is that correct?"

Richard

"YES."

(D'Ann had never complained of back pain, but severe back pain came one night. We went to the emergency ward that night three times before she was finally admitted after even strong drugs would not stop the pain. D'Ann was modest and shy regarding female problems and "private parts" are words I would have expected her to use.)

George Anderson

"She says there was nothing you could do to save her and thanks you for the care, love, and everything you did. She knew from the beginning she was dying and that you admired her for her courage during her illness. She thanks you for holding her when she died. She did not experience any pain and mentioned going to the light. She says Daddy is there with her. There is a male presence which is sending you his love and indicates he thinks well of you. This may be your wife's father.

She says that you must take yourself off the hook, not feel guilty, and get on with your life. She says you had a very good marriage and she loves you very much and knows you love her. She repeats this several times. You had some ups and downs but mostly ups. Again, she knows you love her and she loves you. Your time is not at hand but she will be there waiting for you.

Your wife sends her love to Catherine or Cathy. Does that make sense?"

Richard

"YES."

(I was cradling D'Ann's head in my arms when she died. I kissed her and my tears fell on her cheek. A nurse from Hospice stood by the door.

Charles, D'Ann's father, was a fine man and we liked each other very much. Cathy Burt Campbell is D'Ann's oldest friend dating back to elementary school. They stayed close throughout their lives and D'Ann talked to and saw Cathy during her illness.)

George Anderson

"Your wife sends her love to her mother and your children. She thanks you for praying for her. You talk with your wife, don't you?"

Richard

"YES."

(In Florida, I have a memory room with several large picture collages of D'Ann and our friends in the North and in the South. Often I would sit and pray, meditate, or talk out loud when I looked at D'Ann telling her my thoughts on the day, my activities, and how much I missed her.)

George Anderson

"She indicates she has a very short name. Less than six letters, five no four. Two letters are the same. I see two N's and a D. It doesn't make sense. She says it could be pronounced like a man's name. Do you understand?"

Richard

"NO."

(Rita raised her eyebrows, thinking I was rather dense as immediately she realized Dann equals "Dan." Finally without any help from me, George came up with D'Ann.)

George Anderson

"D'Ann says all your pets are with her. She seems like a very sweet lady and once more she thanks you for a wonderful marriage. You were her best friend and she was yours and she loves you very much. She is holding out a bouquet of white roses to you for your anniversary, which is soon, and your birthday, which is later in the year. She also mentions September."

Richard

(Our anniversary is May 26th, a little over a month away. My birthday is in August and D'Ann's birthday is in September.)

George Anderson

"They are leaving now."

Richard

(Over one-and-one-half-hours had passed.)

Rita and I rose, chatted briefly with George, thanked him, and left the hotel in silence. I remained in a state of wonder, joy, and for the first time in months, at peace with the world and myself. There were no longer doubts in my mind that D'Ann and all my loved ones were fine. I would see them again. I looked at my life and our world from a brand new perspective. I had been given access to a world that in my most optimistic moments I had only hoped might exist. Thanks to George, I believe, I had been given a glimpse of a parallel world. For some reason, a few words by William Shakespeare came to mind. "All the world's a stage and we are but players . . . "

"Yes", I thought, "And we're supposed to play our parts as best we can—I guess that's why we are here but its certainly not easy."

Finally, when we reached the car, Rita and I began to express our feelings. She, too, felt it had been one of the most wonderful experiences of her life. It had changed us both and the implications of the experience would influence the rest of our lives.

Up to that day, I had focused mostly on the material and physical side of life with very little reflection or thought regarding a possible spiritual life. George's relaying of thoughts, feelings and facts from my loved ones that only I could know left me with no choice but to accept the reality that a spiritual world exists. My acceptance of this almost inconceivable concept has changed forever my attitude toward every second, minute, and day I live. As sure as I now am in the spiritual purpose of life and the hereafter, I can understand why anyone and everyone may have their doubts.

Doubting Thomas' probably have always been the large majority of the world's population. Even the holiest and consistently devout have more than likely asked during their lifetimes why their God has forsaken them. Many people, deep down, simply remain unconvinced by the words of the masters as to the spiritual nature of life, our eternal soul, and immortality. Ancient words written or spoken by hundreds of followers thousands of years ago, translated and interpreted differently by thousands convince millions that the true nature of God or the universe is beyond our grasp.

I certainly would have remained a member of this majority if not for my meetings with George Anderson. I would have lived the rest of my life questioning whether or not there was a reason for human existence and wondering if life is simply one roll of the dice. Of course, I could have tried to understand, dissect, and see all the chemical and mechanical operations that make flowers beautiful. I might have learned the muscles, nerves, and synapses that make children and adults smile. Yet, the few questions I might have found answers to would have led to more unknowns. All my days could have been spent looking for answers that are beyond my understanding.

Most of the daily miracles we experience, from a magnificent sunset to the first cry of a newborn, we must accept as the manifestation of a greater power or dismiss it as random chance. I can no longer not believe in miracles simply because I do not understand how they are created.

"You monks, straining day after day to understand what Zen might be, are barking up the wrong tree!
What you can't seem to see is that all is beyond understanding, not just one thing or many things,
but every single thing is fundamentally beyond our understanding.
The Really Real, in its Suchness, is beyond our understanding."

BUTSUGEN, eleventh century Buddhist Monk

Awe precedes faith; it is at the root of faith.
We must grow in awe in order to reach faith.

ABRAHAM JOSHUA HESHCEL

D'Ann and my brother Bob had admonished me to get on with my life. Four hours later when we arrived back in Palm Coast I was determined to do just that, but of course it is easier said than done. Knowing D'Ann was fine helped a great deal, but of course I still missed her terribly and always will. After meeting with George, each day seemed a little bit brighter and the load we all carry after losing a loved one, lighter.

My belief that we are truly spiritual beings is married to my every thought and, I hope, at least to most deeds. However, I must admit that when the golf ball I have willed to fly directly down the middle of the fairway disappears amongst the bordering trees, the spiritual aspect of life is momentarily forgotten.

Life Begins Again

$\mathcal{C}$ h a p t e r IX

I returned to Massachusetts with a much happier heart. My heavy schedule of book signings, watching over Nina, and preparing two houses to be sold did not weigh me down as before. During the year, a lady who was a manufacturer's rep and had sold my books to stores became part of my life. Her name is Judy. She has a son and daughter and two grandchildren. As time passed we became closer.

In January 1999, Judy Gale Smith and I went to Ecuador to meet D'Ann's and my godchildren. We told them Judy and I would be getting married in September. Fredy, Cesar, Pablo, my mother Bee, and mother-in-law Nina, had given us their blessings. It was a wonderful trip from start to finish. Twenty-five members of our Ecuadorian family met us at the airport with a large sign, "WELCOME RICHARD AND JUDY TO ECUADOR—YOUR SECOND HOME." Judy was presented with two dozen long stem red roses.

Two wonderful weeks later, our Ecuadorian friends hired a Mariachi Band to serenade us on the evening of our departure. We bid our large Ecuadorian family a happy—tearful good-bye.

Judy is a very special lady. As I tried to get on with my life, Judy accepted the fact that it was to be a slow process with many emotional ups and downs. Before seeing George Anderson I doubted I would ever get married again. Judy and I enjoyed each other's company and found we had many common interests. I came to love her and her children and grandchildren dearly. Although a spiritual person in her own way, like most people, she had serious doubts as to the ability of anyone being able to communicate with loved ones who have passed, whether it be via George Anderson or someone else. However, I felt if Judy met with George, at least she would understand my spiritual philosophy and the road I am taking with this book.

Judy had lost her mother in 1998. I told her of my experiences and my search during the past three years. She reluctantly agreed to meet with George Anderson, if I could get an appointment. I sent in the request in November of 1998 and we were informed that George could see us the next June. On June 1, 1999 we arrived at the Hampton Inn on Long Island, NY at 3:00 P.M. At 4:45 we went to the lobby and Dianne Vetucci was waiting. Dianne is a friend of George's and helps him when his full time coordinator, Andrew Barone, can't be there. She is a very pleasant lady and we chatted briefly about George. Dianne told us, "George is just as he appears—quiet, unassuming, and not the least affected by the gift he has been given."

She went on to say most of the money he receives goes to the Catholic Church and charities. A little after five, Dianne led us to a suite on the fifth floor to meet with George. I expected to be only an observer. I was very wrong.

As we approached the suite, a family of four was leaving. They were very happy and I overheard them say, "That was wonderful." We entered the living room of the suite. Although I had met George over a year previously, there was no indication of any recognition. We simply shook hands and said we were Richard and Judy. Judy sat on a couch about ten feet from George. After I placed the tape recorder on a table next to him I sat down in an armchair six feet away from George.

George Anderson

"Please just say yes, no, or maybe when I ask you if you understand. There are several presences entering the room. There's a female presence that comes into the room followed by a male and another female.

They are linking you two together. That puzzles me. They are linking you as family but are not coming out and saying you are family. I'm trying to figure why they are doing that."

Richard

(Judy and I had become engaged six months earlier.)

George Anderson speaking to Judy

"There is a female presence that comes up to you that passed on and a male too, right?"

Judy

"YES."

George Anderson

"There is a female presence around you claiming to be your grandmother. She claims to know you. To be honest with you, it seems to be more of a maternal grandmother, so it might be your mom's mother but for whatever reason she is making her presence known. There is also another female presence that comes to you. Does that make sense? Family, yes? And she comes as a mother to you and a male.

And another male. There's actually two, but it seems like it's two different generations. Somebody's older and somebody's younger by generation. Somebody keeps talking about Dad. Do you understand?"

Judy

"YES."

(Judy's father died in a boating accident when Judy was only eleven years old.)

George Anderson

"Somebody claims to be your father's parents. Your father's parents have passed on unless they are one hundred and fifty. Then somebody said your dad is here so it is correct your dad has passed?"

Judy

"YES."

George Anderson

"Okay. So he must be here as well. And a female too. You were close with your grandmother?"

Judy

"YES."

George Anderson

"Who in many ways was like a mom? She keeps embracing you with love in such a motherly sense. She raised you? Yes and no? It's just that she probably was a . . . not like she literally raised you but she was there for you a good deal of your life."

Judy

"YES."

(After Judy's dad died her mother took over their insurance company and Judy spent a lot of time each week with her grandmother who lived only a mile away.)

George Anderson

"She certainly was an influence. She either lived with you or was near-by. It is someone you had a close rapport with. She thanks you for always being there for her when she was on earth. There's an apple over your head so in many ways you were the apple of her eye. Now without explaining, she calls to your mom. Do you understand?"

Judy

"YES."

George Anderson

"She is saying your Mom is with you. Your mother must be with you in a spiritual sense. Now your mother draws very close to you. She comes to you in friendship as well as in motherliness. Your mother keeps telling me she is fine and at peace. She asks that I relate the message to you that she's fine and at peace. She says she and your father are together over there. Does that make sense?"

Judy

"YES."

George Anderson

"Along with your grandparents, so I take it all your grandparents have passed. They seem to be saying they are all there. Your mother brings up the loss of a child? Did she have a miscarriage? Is that correct?"

Judy

"YES."

George Anderson

"I think you would have had a brother. Your mother says if the birth had continued it would have been a son. Your mother says you took care of her. I don't know how but she says you did. It could have been emotionally—its not like you were Florence Nightingale but she says you took care of her. Your father says he could have been closer. Would you agree?"

Judy

"YES."

(Judy's father was in the Navy for her first five years and then when he was discharged after the war, he began his own business which took a lot of his time.)

George Anderson

"Your father wants you to know he always loved you, even if at times he might have had a strange way of showing it. Not that he . . . You didn't have a horrible relationship. It's just at times you needed him and he wasn't there. You pray for them in your own way, yes? Which they certainly thank you for and ask you to continue to pray for them. Your mother says she did not have the easiest life on earth but she thinks she had a fulfilling life."

George Anderson speaking to Richard

"Somebody's around you calling out Dad. The presence has been over there a while. He gives me the impression he can show us around. He also feels he could have been closer. Would you agree?"

Richard

"YES."

(I was surprised because I believed it was my brother Bob coming through again as he did in the first session I had with George. At that time, Bob talked at length about his life, his problems with epilepsy, and the fact we were not as close as maybe we could have been. Since this appointment had been set up for Judy, I had not expected to hear from any members of my family that have passed. I was wrong. It appears spirits know when they will have an opportunity to communicate with loved ones.)

George Anderson

"Again it's not that you had a horrible relationship. That is what he feels but he feels it is understood now anyway. It's like bringing up old news. Right? He indicates he is just touching base to bring it up so that you recognize that it is understood."

Richard

"YES."

(After the first meeting with George, and hearing from Bob, I certainly felt that I was not only closer to my brother, but I understood the torment he endured during his lifelong, physical and emotional, battle with epilepsy.)

George Anderson speaking to Judy and Richard

"The two of you get linked again. Are you very close or something? You're here together as close friends and this could be why you're linked as family. You may not be family by blood but by choice. Does the name Jim mean anything at all to either of you?"

Richard

"YES."

(Jim Fardy was probably dad's best friend. Dad's mother's nephew.)

George Anderson speaking to Richard

"He seems to be around your dad. There is also talk of the loss of a sibling. Does that make sense?"

Richard

"YES."

(My brother Bob passed away at age thirty-seven.)

George Anderson

"I sense a younger presence around you. It could be a younger male like a brother or brother-in-law. He says he is there with your parent. Another presence says he is with your mom. I hear the name Brian?"

Richard

"Not sure."

(My father's name was Edwin and D'Ann's maiden name was O'Brien. I am confused as to where this is leading.)

George Anderson

"Your father is with your mom spiritually. He keeps saying he is with your mom in the spiritual sense as she is still on earth. He tells me your mother should watch where she is walking. She is in okay shape but your father indicates he is around her like a guardian angel. Your father draws closer so I take it they were very close. He was glad he went first because he thinks he would have had a much more difficult time being a widower. Whether your mother believes his message or not, it doesn't matter.

He says just tell her you have heard from him and let her know he's with her. He's emphasizing that he's with her. I'm sure she does miss him and he keeps stating he is near. He also states he will be very close to you on Father's Day."

Richard

"YES."

(My dad was an extremely kind, gentle, and compassionate man but he had tremendous fears. He never went to a dentist, wouldn't drive over

bridges, or through tunnels. Psychologically, I believe he was extremely dependent on my mom. He would never travel more than a few hours away and then only on back roads. He saw his first doctor after his heart attack. He would have had a very difficult time as a widower.)

George Anderson speaking to Judy

"I also keep hearing the name Helen."

Richard

(The only Helen we could think of was my father's mother, Helen Somersby Wainwright but that did not feel right. Especially as Judy's mother's message continued following George's statement. Judy's mother's name, Velma, is so rare I just wonder if George just wasn't able to discern the difference between Helen and Velma.)

George Anderson

"Your mother says she comes to you in dreams but you may not remember. She tells me this is not the first time you're hearing from her. Do you understand why your mother says she hasn't been there that long? I guess she passed not long ago?"

Judy

"YES."

(Judy's mom passed on August 8, 1998.)

George Anderson speaking to Richard

"She says hello to you and says she knew you."

Richard

"YES."

(Judy and I spent several days in California with Velma and her husband, Don, the summer before she died.)

George Anderson speaking to Judy

"Again your mom says hello and sends her love to all the family. Your mother tells me she knew she was going to pass on and is not surprised to be where she is. I see St. Joseph appear and he is the patron of a happy death. She passes in her sleep. She states you never let her down. Do you understand? You never failed her. At the end, to a degree, your hands were tied. There was only so much you could do. You could not save her. Your mother seems like a pretty straightforward woman. She states if it wasn't meant to be she wouldn't have passed on. There is a scheduled time to be born and a scheduled time to pass on. She hooked up with your Dad. He was there first and he must have welcomed her into the light or at least was one of the souls that welcomed her. She still insists that she had a fulfilling life."

(Judy's mother passed away in California. Judy, her brother and sister, and their families visited Velma as much as possible during her last year.)

George Anderson speaking to Richard

"Somebody waltzes in and says Marguerite. She seems to hang around you. She claims she knew your father once and that is why I *(George Anderson)* paid more attention to you. She said, 'Oh no, I know his father.' She seems not to be super close with you but apparently she's coming in to say hello. She considers herself family by emotion. By blood somehow. She says your mother knows her. She comes in motherliness. She'd be like an aunt—something of this nature. She wants to be acknowledged she's here."

Richard

"YES."

(Marguerite Fardy was Jim Fardy's wife—distant relatives but were close emotionally to my folks and me.)

George Anderson speaking to Judy

"A chapter of your life has closed but a new one begins. Your mother talks of you coming . . . I'm going to use a word that I don't want to use the way we would normally think but your mother says you have divorced yourself. You are breaking away from the old and going into the new. You're divorcing from the past or the status quo of your life in the past, opening up new horizons because covered wagons are there in front of you and they represent a new beginning. There's paper piled up around you. Does that mean anything? As part of the change, I take it you work with a lot of paper. I see it piling up all around you. It has to do with your work I am being told."

Judy

"YES."

(Judy was divorced in September, 1994. She worked as a gift manufacturer's rep until 1992 when she began her own company directly representing manufacturers and selling their products to stores in New England. A great deal of paper is generated via mail orders, fax orders, acknowledgements, and constant communication between Judy and her retail accounts and manufacturers.)

George Anderson

"Your mother insists it is rewarding because I also see finance whirling around you. I'm not saying you are a millionaire but definitely finance grows around you. They say your home situation changes. I don't want to say you are moving but your home is changing. There's the birth of a child, which in this case represents a new beginning. Your mother says your home situation is changing and for the better. Your mother keeps saying she is all right. Your mom speaks of children. So I take it you have children?"

Judy

"YES."

(Judy sold the house in 1996 where she and her husband raised their two children.)

George Anderson

"She's saying 'grandchildren' so she must be calling out for her grandchildren." *(Velma had a total of four grandchildren and two great-grandchildren.)*

George Anderson speaking to Richard

"Your father keeps calling out to a Bill/William. He also congratulates him."

Richard

"YES."

(Bill is my brother-in-law. He and my sister celebrated their 40th wedding anniversary a few weeks prior to this discernment and Bill had recently retired.)

George Anderson

"There's a Bob/Robert. He's with your dad so he must have passed on. I don't know but he seems to like you very much because he is around you at times like a guardian angel. Is there a reason why? He is bringing up your mother's health. Has she been having trouble with her health?"

Richard

"YES."

(Bob communicated for a long time in the first discernment and I think got a lot off his chest—so to speak. As strange as it may sound we are probably closer now than when Bob was living on earth. At ninety-one my mom has assorted health problems but with weekly help and assistance from my sister, Nancy, and her family, she is able to live in her own apartment.)

George Anderson

"She is in okay shape because they are not telling me anything you don't know already. No new news but they're saying keep alert to her health. If she honestly doesn't feel right get it checked. But again, I get the feeling you just have to live with it. She's told to watch her walking. Your father says she is in familiar surroundings. It could be a home or whatever."

Richard

"YES."

(Since the discernment mom has had several falls inside and outside her condo.)

George Anderson speaking to Judy

"Your mother says you have come a long way. Yeah, because I see the Virginia Slims lady over your head. I mean, your life was not completely horrible but you have gone through lessons and it has been happier in the past five years than it has ever been. I keep seeing you in the driver's seat so apparently you have a greater sense of control. Your mom is around you playing the guardian angel.

The Holy Spirit is over your head, which has nothing to do with religion. It's a symbol that the life is blessed. She's stating that she's all right and in a happy place. Your life is going into a cycle of a new beginning. Again things have been divorced and change has come in—a new direction. There's more a sense of balance and you know where you are going."

Judy

"YES."

George Anderson speaking to Richard

"It is the same with you. The last few years might not have been the easiest. A chapter of your life closed and a new one began. The status quo was upset. You too have come a long way. Your father just wants you to know he was around you—helping you help yourself. You've surmounted many obstacles—not minor ones. You've grown from the experience even though it was not a happy or easy time. He says watch your drinking. He's not saying you are an alcoholic so there must be a reason for saying it. You know it disagrees with you."

Richard

"YES."

(Over twenty years ago in Ecuador I contracted Non-A/Non-B hepatitis. Although my liver function hovers around normal, I have been told by doctors to be very careful with alcohol even though over the years I drank very little.)

George Anderson speaking to Judy

"A Henry comes into the room. Somebody's walked into the room and just told me to say the name Henry. He states he is family. He appears like a father or grandfather in nature. He knows your parents. Again your mother brings up the loss of a child so she must have miscarried. I think it would have been a brother and she keeps talking about his soul being there. I see animals and children around you. Does that mean anything?"

Judy

"YES."

(One of Judy's grandfathers was a Henry. Judy's mother did have a miscarriage. Judy has two children and had a number of pets including three dogs, rabbits, and a cockatiel. Now she has two additional grandchildren, and of course, has gotten to know D'Ann's and my children along with our cat, Consuelo. Judy also helps me with book signings, and of course, there is contact with children on those occasions.)

George Anderson speaking to Richard

"There is a Sal or Al around your Dad claiming to be Uncle Al. Passed on?"

Richard

"YES."

(My first uncle to pass was Uncle Al. My mother's brother.)

George Anderson

"Yeah, because he seemed to lose his patience, which is okay. He got through clearly enough. I'm glad. I couldn't tell if I heard Sal or Al. He said, 'no, it's Al.' He said, 'yes, yes, say its Uncle Al.' So I did. He claims he is with your dad and he knows your mother."

George Anderson speaking to Judy

"A man came in the room and seemed to disappear. I heard the name Arthur coming in your direction. Passed on? Arthur? He didn't pressure me but seemed to drift in your direction so it figured he passed on?"

Judy

"YES."

(One of Judy's grandfathers was Arthur.)

George Anderson

"He states he is family. He doesn't give me the impression he is super close to you but he could have been. Well, it's good you recalled him right away. He is here with your parents. There's fatherlyness about him. He says his wife is with him. He wants you to know the two of them are together. Do you own a pet because I am seeing animals around you? Your mother said pets that passed on are with her. I see a cat too. It could be a symbol but apparently the pets that you lost must be there with her."

(Judy and her parents have had many pets.)

George Anderson speaking to Richard

"Somebody in the room is singing 'Danny Boy'. Does that make sense? It can be the clue to the name Daniel but it seems to be more with you. I mean, it can represent Irish heritage but the song came in and seemed to be more at you and involved with the name Daniel. I don't know what else to do with it."

Richard

"Not sure."

(I hadn't expected to hear from D'Ann again but her maiden name was O'Brien and D'Ann is not far from Daniel. I also remembered that in the first discernment D'Ann told George her name could be pronounced like a man's name—DANN. I could only wait to confirm or deny.)

George Anderson

"Your father says make sure you're getting enough rest. It's like you're sleeping but not resting. Your schedule is all whacked up or something. I *(George Anderson)* feel like I'm not calming down as well as

I should. There's a lot of stress around you in your work. Is this true? I mean, you're not going to jump off the Brooklyn Bridge but he speaks of more demand coming to you. I keep seeing two pieces of pie—like I'm doing one job but handling something else."

Richard

"YES."

(I have had a problem with esophageal reflux for a number of years and find it difficult to get a full and deep sleep. At this point in my life, I am working on two books, have a full signing schedule ahead of me this summer, and Judy and I are working on our wedding plans for this September along with allocating time with our families. My mom (91) and mother-in-law (94) are living and we try to share our lives with them. I don't believe I am busier then anybody else but for me, my plate, I feel, holds a large helping.)

George Anderson

"Why is there talk of a wife going out of your life? Does that make sense?"

Richard

"YES."

George Anderson

"Strange way to put it. They keep bringing up your wife. Do you understand?"

Richard

"YES."

George Anderson

"So it is correct your wife passed on. Okay, that's why they . . . Your parent keeps bringing it up. Now somebody is talking about the loss of a daughter . . . daughter-in-law. I mean your dad is referring to her as a daughter-in-law. I just thought I would ask if you lost a sister and he said, no, no, no, you don't understand it yet. It's apparently your wife, his daughter-in-law. There is also a lot of writing around you. Does that make sense?"

Richard

"YES."

George Anderson

"Because your wife has all these books piled up around you. She says you are published. You are published?"

Richard

"YES."

George Anderson

"Okay, you don't write just for the hell of it. It has meaning behind it. Your wife draws close to you not only as a wife but also as a good friend. *(George laughs)*. I didn't mean to laugh but she says she has been here from the beginning but got caught in the shuffle. Because she says, remember when I said a male presence comes into the room, then a wife and another female follows. They had to decide who was to go first. Your wife says she decided to let the others go before her. She's joking but says to save the best for last. Your wife sensed that Judy needed to hear from her mom so she took a back seat so Judy would have a chance to hear from her mom and grandmother. Then she came forward. Your wife must have had a big heart. You pray for her in your own way?"

Richard

"YES."

George Anderson

"She certainly thanks you for it and asks you to please continue. She says you have started to get on with your life and she's glad. For awhile you kind of buried yourself alive. Your life is getting better and better and she extends gladness from the hereafter. It sounds as if you are doing the right thing and she agrees because you have to go on with your life. She knows it is difficult being a widower, especially since you and she had a very close relationship.

If one of you had to go, you probably thought it would be you. You could have gone first but she states you're not supposed to be there yet. You still have things to fulfill in your lifetime and that is why you are where you are. There are also children around you. Does that make sense?

Richard

"YES."

(In addition to D'Ann's and my godchildren that remain close, our first goddaughter, Maria Augusta, will be coming to live with Judy and me in 2000). I have also become close to Judy's two children and her grandchildren. In addition, I meet a lot of children at book signings and when I speak with young people at schools.)

George Anderson

"As part of your work? Indirectly? It's not that you work directly with children but you do as a writer. I see Charles Dickens over your head. Does that make sense? I'm not saying you write on social issues like he did but you are recognized in your arena. He would be recognized for ***GREAT EXPECTATIONS*** and you are recognized for what you do. Your wife is calling Deanna or Diana. Does that make sense?"

Richard

"YES."

(In my books, I have attempted to focus on many of life's experiences and social issues including courage, love, prejudice, cultural differences, friendship, adoption, spirituality, homelessness, death, fears, perseverance, integrity, sharing, etc.)

George Anderson

"I keep hearing Deanna but I'm probably pronouncing it wrong. I keep hearing the name. She's saying I have to stop after the D, so she is saying D Ann."

Richard

"YES."

George Anderson

"Her name is something like Deanne. It keeps sounding like she's saying to me Deanne, Deanne. She's telling me to pronounce it D-Ann. *(George looks at Judy)*. Oh, she is saying hello to you. She says hello from the hereafter. She keeps calling Richard and making it into a diminutive. Make sense?"

Richard

"YES."

(During our life together our friends called us Dick and Dee.)

George Anderson

"She says since you began going on with your life that you are happier. For a while you were embalmed, but your wife is not unsympathetic to what you have gone through, but you have no choice. You have to go on with your life. She thanks you for being good to her on earth and taking care of her. You could not save her. And she says it is not your fault she passed on. What you and she shared together was special for that time and always will be. She says, 'We'll meet again' and she loves you unconditionally and wants you to be happy in your life.

She jokes. 'There is no jealousy over here. If you fall in love with someone else it doesn't mean you must decide which wife to go to when you pass. It doesn't work that way. She says everybody loves unconditionally and sees from the hereafter the purpose and fulfillment of everyone's life.' She certainly understands what you are going through. She keeps putting a big D in front of me. So it's the first letter of her name or she is sometimes called Dee. I have the impression you could always depend on her to tell it like it is. She's not a BS artist. Are you living in two places?"

Richard

"YES."

(For the past three years, I often thought about what D'Ann's attitude would be regarding my remarriage and whether or not I should enter into another marriage after having had a wonderful marriage with D'Ann. Judy and I live in Scituate, Massachusetts six months a year and six months in Palm Coast, Florida.)

George Anderson

"You may be spending more time in one, going back and forth, but eventually, up ahead, one place will dominate. You're also enlarging your capacities in your writing. Even though you are in a particular area right now, your wife shows me the trunk of a tree that sprouts branches which means you will go into other subjects maintaining your basic philosophy represented by the trunk of the tree. Let's say you write something orientated for children now. You may write something out of that arena but still maintain the trunk of what you do. Your wife calls to family. Do you know the family she means?"

Richard

"YES."

(Knowing D'Ann, she would be referring to our godchildren, her mother, our relatives, and all our friends that she loved so much. With this book, I am certainly attempting to write something very different than

my previous books and the tree analogy is especially appropriate as "I am going out on a limb with this one.")

George Anderson

"She's saying that she's alright and in a happy place. I (*George Anderson*) am intrigued why she was here at the beginning and yet she stepped aside and let others come through first. She jokes again—best for last."

George Anderson speaking to Judy

"I hear an Al or Adam . . . it's around your mom. She was talking about somebody, Anne or Abby, being there with that name. She shows me the old neighborhood so it's probably from the past or somebody that she might have known in the old neighborhood."

Judy

"NO."

(Judy can't remember anyone with those names in her mother's life. Judy's mother Velma was sometimes called "Vel.")

George Anderson speaking to Richard

"Again your wife expresses that she's glad that you're going on with your life. You need to be nurtured and need company. There is always hesitation, should I or shouldn't I, and what she says is that you should. She wants you to be happy in whatever endeavor or direction your life goes. I see grace written over your head, which is a symbol of blessings in this case. Now, I keep seeing St. Agatha appear. St. Agatha normally means a woman had something in the cancer family."

Richard

"YES."

George Anderson

"Yes, because your wife keeps telling me to pay attention to the symbol. She had cancer. She says it kind of sneaked up on her. Like all of a sudden it's there although she probably had it for quite a while and she didn't know it. Anyway, it happened and even though she tried to get well, it wasn't supposed to be. She certainly put up a courageous struggle but she was supposed to pass on. Even though, as we understand it, she had a short life, she feels she had a happy life, a fulfilling life and accomplished many things. She states to you that it was better to have the time you did together than never at all."

George Anderson speaking to Judy

"A Mary comes in. Does that make sense? Your grandmother's generation."

Judy

"NO."

(Judy cannot recall any Mary who was close to her grandmother.)

George Anderson

"Somebody keeps talking and saying that you're ending a marriage. Do you understand?"

Judy

"YES."

George Anderson

"A separation, but in this case not due to a death. You're not a widow. They keep telling me it is not the same as the gentleman. It happened. Again they are telling me you divorced yourself, you separated, but your mother says it is for the better. Your mother and father state the chances are you have never been happier. You are back in the driver's seat and what they are saying is that the past is water under the bridge. You're supposed to go through whatever you've experienced and then go in a new direction."

George Anderson speaking to Richard

"I think your wife was speaking again. Again, I see birth in front of you, representing a new direction. New things happening in your life in regards to career and personal life. There might have been a sense of emptiness for awhile or things just on plateau, but now things begin to go in a new and challenging direction. They are fading out and leaving."

(Over one hour had passed.)

I felt truly elated hearing from D'Ann and other family members again. I was convinced that Judy's mother, grandmother, and grandfathers had come through, but I had previously crossed the bridge of believing that George was truly able to serve as a receiver of messages from loved ones. On the other hand, Judy continued to ponder and question the experience. Judy's mother's name, Velma, did not come through loud and clear. Yet George's messages from Judy's "mother and grandmother" were on target and her two grandfather's names were correct.

I will be forever indebted to Judy's willingness and courage to be part of this book, and for her support and encouragement as I complete this literary journey. Sharing our personal lives with strangers or (as Will Rogers said, "friends we haven't met") is not easy.

Before I met with George, even though I had read all his books, I probably would have taken the position that what George does is, yes, amazing but scientifically inexplicable and so unacceptable. Now my position is, even though George and other credible mediums' abilities are inexplicable, (to them as well as myself), "the evidence presented rings true to me" so I accept it.

Quite early in life I became an honorary Missourian. When it came to religious or spiritual faith I fell in with the "Show me— prove it!" faithful. Yet, I had tremendous faith in flipping on light switches and appliances though I had no idea how electricity worked. I boarded airplanes with confidence knowing nothing about aeronautics and I type these words without a clue as to the basic nature of this computer. Though I understand on a simplistic level some of the theories and ideas of the world's foremost scientists my acceptance is closer to blind faith than knowledge. Unashamedly, I realize I am unable to grasp what millions probably can. Consequently, for me to extrapolate from my limited experience, intellect, and knowledge, the mechanics of creation is obviously mission impossible. How the human soul relates to time and space and the nature of other dimensions will remain a mystery to me during this lifetime. Eventually I will learn more but for the moment I am extremely grateful to George for making it possible for me to receive a glimpse of eternity.

All, all for immortality,
Love like the light silently wrapping all.

WALT WHITMAN

I do not think seventy years is the
time of man or woman . . .
Nor that years will ever stop the
existence of me or any one else.

WALT WHITMAN

There are two ways to be fooled. One is to believe
what isn't true; the other is to refuse to believe what is true.

SOREN KIERKEGAARD

Windmills in my Mind

$\mathcal{C}$ h a p t e r X

Even though I was convinced in the reality of the discernments with George Anderson, I knew sharing these experiences with others would be a risky business. I certainly didn't consider chronicling this segment of my spiritual journey in the form of a book. My first tentative disclosure of my meeting with George Anderson was sending copies of the first discernment to members of my family and a few close friends. I knew my family couldn't disown me, and I hoped my incredulous friends would simply chock it up to either a latent mid-life crisis or temporary insanity.

As time went by, occasionally and hesitantly, I mentioned my experiences to friends and would bring up Dr. Moody's book *LIFE AFTER LIFE*. Much to my surprise, I learned several of my friends had had near-death experiences but they had never mentioned them as they felt no one would believe their experiences. The first was a close friend of over thirty years who told me that during an operation she had left her body and went toward a bright white light.

Another friend playing golf was stung by a bee and went into anaphylactic shock. While draped over the golf cart and being rushed to the clubhouse, she found herself out of her body moving toward a bright light. Her deceased mother appeared and lovingly, simply told her daughter, "it is not your time." After an anti-histamine shot from a doctor member, who just happened to be in the clubhouse, my friend awoke.

Since I began this book, I have met at least ten people (much more normal than I) who have shared near-death and spiritual experiences.

One such lady was Janice. She worked for me creating and handling sales of my books on E-bay. As we worked together we became friends. I told her of this book and Janice told me this story. After a risky operation while she was in the ICU, her husband Joe, who had died, appeared during a crisis. He reassured her that she was going to make it. She commented, "Since that experience, my life has changed in many ways. I don't sweat the small stuff. I try to love more each day. Someday, Dick, I'll tell you the rest of my "other-side stories: my grandfather's visit, my friend's whisper, my brother's practical jokes, my brother-in-law's musical message, and the different ways people have sent messages to me after they died."

Fran who lives in Connecticut discovered years ago that often when she was praying for a particular person who had passed on she would be directed to write a message. The words seemed to flow directly to her hand. When you look at what she has written, it appears to be simply a stream of words until the appropriate punctuation is inserted. The individuals, who were the recipients of these messages, authenticate them from specific personal information contained in the message. She has no idea how or why she has come to have this ability. Sharing what she receives has brought comfort to hundreds who remain behind.

Several years ago, a television special presented a two-hour program on spirituality, mediums, and scientific attempts to find evidence that there is life after death. There were many anecdotal reports by individuals who told of personal spiritual experiences with loved-ones. According to the narrator, Linda Ellerby, over 50 million people across the world have reported spiritual—paranormal experiences. During the program, mediums such as George Anderson, John Edwards, and others conducted readings for individuals that proved to be accurate. This special program documented the first scientific study ever done regarding the ability of anyone to communicate with those in the hereafter. The study was done at the University of Arizona. Five mediums, including George Anderson, met one at a time, with a woman hidden from view. They had never seen or heard of the woman who sat on the other side of a curtain. Each medium spent approximately fifteen minutes with her relating images and messages they received. The mediums' comments were to be acknowledged with only a Yes or No.

All five received the message that the woman had lost a son who had taken his own life with the use of a firearm. Her son conveyed why he took his life but suggested it was a mistake. A family dog played a major role in both the mother and son's life. The mediums relayed many aspects of his life while on earth. All the mediums basically received the same information, and according to the mother the information could only have come from her son.

One evening during the past year, Judy was watching a program on the *Lifetime* channel called *Beyond Chance*. Neither one of us had heard it advertised. It was a story about two families that had lost their teen daughters, one year apart, during separate equestrian competitions. The girls had been very close friends. Of course, both families were devastated by their losses and eventually someone recommended they see George Anderson. The two sets of parents met separately with George. The sessions were taped. Both parents and George swore this was their first meeting. The messages George received zeroed right in on the childrens' passing. The daughters explained specific details of their deaths that the parents and medical community had only wondered about. The information received convinced both sets of parents that they had truly heard from their daughters who were not only well but had "hooked up" in the next dimension.

For anyone interested in psychic phenomena there is now a considerable body of credible literature, documentaries, and personal testimony to evaluate. As I have said, my experiences with George Anderson have given me peace of mind and a belief that D'Ann, my father, and brother, along with all our loved ones who have passed, are well and happy. And when the time comes, they will be waiting to lead me to the light. (At least, I hope someone will have time to show me the way as I get lost easily on earth and imagine without help I would go in circles forever in the next dimension.) To quote, Elisabeth Kubler-Ross, "Death does not exist—only a transition from life to afterlife."

Most of my life, I have played the devil's advocate and questioned almost everything. Now I believe my most important questions have been answered. Yet, answers always seem to lead to more questions. When I think about George's gift and others who have psychic abilities, the question arises, why not me? Why can't souls communicate with me? Why, throughout history, have some people had visions and special abilities to communicate with the hereafter and not everyone? Why was a carpenter chosen, a man like Edgar Cayce who seemed to have been born an average human being, and spiritual masters whose lives and paranormal abilities have stood the test of time? No one can answer these questions. However, I can ask the same questions when I see or read about extraordinarily talented, compassionate, and wise human beings I greatly admire. My guess is that we are to use what gifts we have been given as best we can and share them with those who become part of our lives.

After the sessions with George, I wanted to hear more, lots more. I wanted to hear from people who I knew well and loved. I wanted a detailed description of the hereafter. I wanted spirits to tell me how they recognize each other. I wanted to know why my Uncle Charlie, who died last year, didn't stop by to say hello. We were close. Why couldn't the spirits stay longer? Why only an hour or hour-and-a-half? Why couldn't they stay for three hours or three days? No one knows but the answers will be given to us someday.

With crackers and water every few hours, I would have been happy for a week to ask questions and listen to the answers. Yet, I realize, I probably had been given much more than I deserved by souls who love me. George sees up to six people a day. The drain on his mental energy level must be tremendous. Many of my questions have been answered by reading of other people's discernments, and by others who have written of their personal spiritual experiences.

George Anderson has been given a gift, but he does not have an easy task. He has the ability to receive messages from those who have passed, but the form of communication is obviously not as straight forward as a telephone connection, a telegram, or e-mail. George has to interpret the symbols he sees and the emotions he feels. He tries to understand how the signs he sees, words he hears in his mind, and feelings he experiences relate to the individual who has come to see him without asking questions. It must be difficult for George to interpret and separate all the emotional energy coming from the spirit of the loved one(s) as well as the bereaved in the room who are hanging on George's every word. The emotions George feels and symbols he sees may be directed toward the individuals who have come to meet with George or be connected to the life of the spirit. Considering the nature of the communication, his accuracy is amazing; but of course, the idea that anyone has this gift is mind-boggling.

George Anderson is correct better than 90% of the time interpreting what he hears and sees mentally during discernments. Other writers referring to his ability have written, "What accolades and salary would a professional baseball player get if he could hit a home run 90% of his times at bat?"

George has a great gift, which he shares. I believe each one of us has gifts we can share. At a book signing, a lady in line, leaning on a single crutch, pushed a wheelchair with a child in it and waited patiently. Although, I could see them peripherally, I couldn't go any faster. I spend a few personal moments with each customer. I thanked my customer, stood up, and waited while the wheelchair rolled in front of me. The bent over lady introduced herself and her very small eight-year old cerebral palsied daughter, whose twinkling eyes and beatific smile seemed greatly at odds with her frail, poorly functioning body. The child spoke and her words flowed. She was very articulate and read well beyond her years. According to her mother, her daughter also possessed a photographic memory.

We chatted as I signed several books and as I listened to their story I experienced a feeling of guilt for being whole. The mother appeared to be a happy and positive person, and I innocently asked, if one day—some day—she would be able to do without the crutch.

She replied, "Afraid not—I was born with Spina Bifida."

I blurted out in a whisper, "How do you do it?"

The mother and daughter smiled in unison and the mother said, "We simply live one day at a time and count our blessings."

I finished signing the books, patted the woman's shoulder, and reached out to hold the child's hand.

"You have made my day." I told them.

The person who had been behind them had been equally moved and we stood mesmerized as the mother laboriously pushed her daughter toward the exit. I often think of that meeting and all the lives the mother and daughter will touch. How many of us are able to say we have always given our best considering our abilities and situation. In truth, I remain in awe of every human being I see, meet, or read about. Especially those who are physically challenged, homeless, infirm, unwanted, face seemingly insurmountable obstacles, or are unloved. I wonder, how do they cope? Could I do half as well? I doubt it.

Every year I watch, mesmerized by the talents and courage of the Para Olympic and Special Olympic competitors. Sometimes I imagine that God daily sits in the bleachers and watches our planet's population—"Earth's Olympic Team"—hoping each one of us, with our disabilities and weaknesses, will simply give life our best shot.

THE HEREAFTER

As a youngster, I was comforted with the knowledge that I had a strong back as I expected to need it some day shoveling coal "down below." It appears my childhood vision of heaven and hell was off the mark. Adult readings and experiences have led me away from the youthful fancy of a heaven filled with prohibited delights, which are found on earth, to a place where there is only love and joy. Our hell is what we create on earth and possibly, after death, when we review our life, we will see that sometimes we could have acted better. Yet, even then, we will forgive ourselves and continue to grow spiritually.

Many, many years ago, in my mind, God appeared as a towering ancient white old man in a gossamer robe holding a golden staff. As I grew older, my male and especially female friends, along with my wife, shattered that idea with simple, but fervent logic. Now, I believe the Creator may be in any form it desires and it may be eons before my spiritual growth reaches the point where I will be able to approach or understand this awesome power.

Through personal spiritual experiences and reading of hundreds of discernments by mediums, I believe we are given some information on conditions in the hereafter and the attitudes of souls toward certain aspects of human life. Below are some of my thoughts and interpretations regarding the hereafter, based on my discernments with George Anderson and his and other mediums' messages received from thousands of souls who have come through during discernments and readings.

1. Our loved ones are alive.

2. Our loved ones continue to grow spiritually.

3. Our loved ones are aware of our emotional and physical health and continue to love us.

4. Our loved ones watch over us and do as much as possible to aid us on our spiritual journey here on earth. Bob

claimed to be my guardian angel. Judy's mother is watching over her. I gather we all have guardian angels but none have the power to stop us from hurting ourselves or others.

5. Our loved ones did not suffer in any way during the transition from the physical body to a spiritual existence.

6. Our loved ones do not suffer from the ailments or disabilities they had on earth. They are whole in the complete sense including mental abilities, which they might have lacked on earth. My brother Bob pointed this out several times.

7. Our loved ones are happy in the hereafter. It is a beautiful place.

8. Pets we have loved on earth are with us in the hereafter.

9. Our loved ones want us to go on with our lives and complete the work we were sent to do.

10. We are told that in the hereafter there is no jealousy or hate and that we will be welcomed in love when it is our time to join them. D'Ann emphasized this point during our second reunion. We should not be concerned whether we were happily married, divorced, remarried, or estranged from people we loved. No one is waiting for us with a heavenly hatchet—only unconditional love.

11. There is no reason to fear death. We are simply making a transition, and our loved ones will be waiting to welcome us.

12. Spirits are aware of our daily lives as they always arrive for a discernment or reading whether it is with George Anderson or other individuals who have the gift of discerning.

13. We are not to feel guilty that we could not save or protect a loved one from passing.

14. Our loved ones ask us to continue to pray for them. They indicate that it not only means a lot to them but helps them as they continue their spiritual growth.

15. Souls stress we are here to learn various spiritual lessons, sometimes those lessons are difficult.

16. Judgement will come after we pass when we review our own life. We are spiritually comforted or helped "to see" during this review. The judgement will be ours alone.

THE HEREAFTER
Described By Residents

It appears a very general idea of the hereafter can be created from statements made by souls through mediums as well as from personal experiences. Heaven, it seems, is quite different than my childhood-vision. The hereafter sounds like a pretty good place. It is a place where we are able to create what we envision, in regard to a person or place. We see our loved ones as we want to remember them. We continue to grow spiritually.

1. Our souls do not become God-like after death—we are part of God. We continue to work on our spiritual growth in the hereafter. The hereafter is a place of indescribable beauty, joy, and love.

2. Souls have jobs to do in the hereafter, taking care of animals, helping newly passed children, or assisting other souls to adjust and grow.

3. Souls who took their own lives indicate that it was a mistake. Although the soul is not punished, the soul in the hereafter realizes that it should have remained on earth and faced the challenges that led to the suicide and continued its spiritual journey. Shortening life in this maner, souls indicate, adds to the work they must do in the hereafter. Do the souls of individuals who end their lives due to severe health problems feel this way too? That is not clear.

4. Since spirits can communicate and sometimes indicate their presence, the spirit world appears to be simply another dimension. It appears that spirits may travel faster than even the speed of light, the universe is their domain. Yet, they often state that they are closer to us than we can imagine—hence the title for this book.

5. Spirits have the ability to recognize one another. What form we take in the hereafter appears to be an amorphous one yet is easily recognizable for loved ones.

6. Spirits seem to suggest that formalized religion is fine and is very important for some people, but it is not the only path an individual can take to develop a spiritual life. People who pray, meditate, and are able to maintain a spiritual consciousness every moment of the day, grow closer to the Light and the Creator.

7. Souls indicate there is no hell as indicated by some religions. Our behavior on earth determines where we are on the spiritual ladder moving toward the Light in the hereafter.

8. Spirits mention an initial life review after having passed, which includes actions that brought pain to others as well as the good works and love given during the lifetime.

9. As to reincarnation, spirits indicate past lives we may have experienced were to learn specific spiritual lessons as is the life we are living today. Our present life is what counts. In this regard, George Anderson has never had any indication from souls that we are ever reincarnated in any other species. This throws cold water on my hope to return one day as a Golden Labrador.

10. Sometimes, souls that hurt people while they were on earth ask for forgiveness during discernments.

11. Souls ask us to forgive people who have hurt us, whether emotionally, with words, or by deeds. We are even asked to forgive a person who took another's life. Souls understand the latter is very difficult but it is one of our spiritual challenges. They have forgiven the perpetrator. Souls stress forgiving and loving everyone is what we should do, as difficult as it sometimes is.

12. Our birth and death are determined by the lessons we are here to learn and the work we are to do. We do have free choice and can detour from the path if we wish. Accidents do happen so our lives may be shortened.

Does Anything Matter ?

Does Everything Matter ?

Chapter XI

————◆————

The 1968 Olympics were held in Mexico City. Late in the afternoon the world's finest marathoners started their 26 mile run in the sun urged on by the cheers of thousands of fans who had packed the stadium for this event. A little over two hours later, the winner came through the stadium entrance receiving a champion's welcome by the throng. In small groups, ones and twos, tired runners entered the stadium during the next hour as the shadows lengthened. With little light remaining and only a handful of spectators present, a lone runner hobbled through the entrance at the far end of the stadium. His knees were bandaged and dried blood covered his calves. Bent over, limping, and obviously in pain, he completed his final lap to finish his 26 miles as the tiny crowd politely applauded and stared.

Amongst the few onlookers was a reporter. He climbed down onto the field and approached the runner—John Stephen Akhwari of Tanzania. With notebook in hand, he asked John Stephen Akhwari why he had continued to run when it was obvious hours ago, that he had no chance of winning. The exhausted Olympian slowly raised his head and at first appeared perplexed by the question. Finally he answered: "My country did not send me to Mexico City to start the race. They sent me to finish."

"STARVATION RETURNS TO ETHIOPIA"
"TWA FLIGHT 800 CRASHES—ALL LOST AT SEA"
"TERRORISTS BLOW UP EMBASSY—HUGE LOSS OF LIFE"
"GLOBAL WARMING IRREVERSIBLE"
"FOUR TEENS DIE IN PROM ACCIDENT"

"POLLUTION AND POPULATION GROWING FASTER THAN TECHNOLOGY"
"CANCER AND MEDICAL CURES ONLY FOR THE FEW WHO CAN AFFORD TREATMENT"

Whether listening to the radio, watching television, surfing the local newspaper or the web, we are bombarded hourly, 365 days a year, with bad news. The terrible consequences of national wild-fires, droughts, and a multitude of tragedies are personally shared with families who have been directly devastated. Starving children and adults speak to us through television and their sunken eyes along with the words of imploring compassionate volunteers. And in our own families personal losses come too often.

It is easy to become discouraged and pessimistic regarding what the future will hold for our children and our children's children.

Yet amongst all this dreadful news, we hear of medical discoveries which eventually may be able to help thousands. We read of individuals whose courage and love have changed and improved the lives of others—one person or many people. We celebrate moments of joy and optimism stimulated by personal achievements and acts of love by those near and dear to us as well as those we hear of in distant lands.

When we watch the Olympics we marvel as many of the most skilled athletes on the planet demonstrate the highest levels of skills in various events. Their years of dedication, sacrifice by themselves and their families, their overcoming the physical and psychological challenges of their sports in order to compete at the highest level, has to give us hope, that when this type of talent is focused on the world's problems, answers will be found. The above statement equally applies to millions of young people in the world who are striving to be the best in their fields whether it be medicine, science, business, education, social work, etc.

Sadly, we more often than not hear of the inhumanity of man towards man rather than the millions of good deeds, sharing, and acts of love that are given unconditionally each day by our neighbors. We have the right and reason to hope that the finest qualities of the human soul will eventually govern and watch over our fragile planet. Surely there are those with the wisdom, courage, and spirituality required to find solutions for the problems of over-population, the continual depletion of our planet's natural resources, worldwide pollution, and the sharing and husbanding of our earth's resources.

How long our planet will survive depends on our collective actions as humans. Earth may continue to exist as an inhabited planet for another millennium or one thousand millenniums. Eventually life will probably cease to exist on earth because of the demise of our sun.

So does anything really matter? Of course it does. We want the world to be even a better place for our children and our children's children. I believe everything we do as individuals truly does matter. Not simply because of what we hope to leave to those who will come after us, but because our spiritual life will continue long after our planet earth is gone. My guess is that we may have more opportunities on this planet or others to continue our spiritual growth. Everything we do impacts our spiritual growth. What we do here on earth, it appears, determines where we will find ourselves in the next dimension on the spiritual ladder. I'm hoping my effort this trip will at least excuse me from working nights.

We are here to learn, to share, and to love everyone—as tough as it sounds. Every act of kindness or love—a smile, helping hand, compliment, compassion, and understanding—with a friend, family member, employee, or stranger will, in some way, change the life of the recipient. A few words or a simple gesture at the right moment may move another's life in a positive direction. Everything we do has an effect on ourselves, everyone on our planet, and our universe. Everything we do does matter. We have not been sent here simply to start a race but to finish it as best we can.

Reflections

$\mathcal{C}h\ a\ p\ t\ e\ r$ XII

There is little more I can add from the discernments or my memory. As George Anderson said, "Knowing our loved ones are still 'alive and well' may bring us a sense of peace." Yet our grieving for those who have passed will remain. We miss them as we would friends and relatives in a distant land, a land where inhabitants may transmit messages that we often do not comprehend or recognize. Nevertheless, as they proceed on their spiritual journey, they continue to love and watch over us until we are reunited.

I believe the following poem I mailed to all of our friends who sent condolences to Nina and myself beautifully expresses my belief in our life after death . . .

THE SHIP

We are standing upon the seashore . . . A ship
Spreads her white sails to the morning breeze, and
Starts for the blue ocean. She is the object of beauty
And strength and I stand and watch her until at
Length she is only a ribbon of white cloud just where
The sea and sky come to mingle with each other.
Then someone at my side says, "There! She's Gone!"

Gone Where?

Gone from my sight, that is all. She is just as large
In mast and hull and spar as she was when she left
My side, and just as able to bear her load of living
Freight—to the place of destination . . . Her diminished
Size is in me—not in her—and just at the
Moment when someone at my side says, "There!
She's Gone!" other eyes are watching for her coming
On the Other Side and other voices are ready to take
Up the glad shout, "There! She comes!"

And that is what we call—Dying.

COL. DAVID MARCUS, U.S.A.

"No where either with more quiet or more freedom from trouble does a man retire than into his own soul . . ."

MARCUS AURELIUS ANTONIUS
ROMAN EMPEROR, 121-180 AD

During the last few years I have tried, not always successfully, to set aside time each day to meditate, ponder, or read works relating to life. I often muse over the meetings with George Anderson and the spiritual experiences of others through the ages past and yesterday. I wonder about the contribution I am expected to make during the rest my life.

My belief that D'Ann and all our loved ones continue to exist is unshakeable. I am indeed thankful to have met Judy as our union has brought even more love into my life. I love her dearly and her wonderful family, her children, and relatives, very much. My god-daughter, Maria Augusta, finally was able to come to the U.S. to study and has become part of our growing family. My life is whole once again. I have been truly blessed.

Today, I look at the world, personal relationships, and each individual differently than I did before D'Ann's passing. Every living creature deserves my compassion and love. I often wonder what would happen if everyone believed that this life is a spiritual journey? Would that knowledge change the way of living and behaving of a large number of human beings?

Could there truly be a heaven on earth?

As much as I would like to believe that the collective spirituality of the world is growing, we obviously, as a species have a long way to go if life on this planet is to survive and we are to become highly evolved beings. I believe God created us as parts of His/Her

Being to experience and remember our spiritual nature. We grow slowly, spiritually through observation, reflection, meditation, and the joys and sorrows of life. These experiences help us remember the true nature of our soul, and our relationship with the Creator becomes closer. As we begin to perceive and accept that God is constantly around us and within us, we become closer to our eternal true spiritual being.

As humans, we are just beginning to scientifically study man's consciousness and the relationship between the physical and psychic world. However, I imagine even with support from the scientific community, a *New York Times* headline claiming ***"EVIDENCE OF THE HEREAFTER DISCOVERED"*** would not produce a rapid shift in the spiritual beliefs and daily behavior of the majority of our planet's inhabitants.

I believe God, our loved ones who have passed on, our guardian angels, and messengers here on earth attempt in various ways to provide us with knowledge of the "real world" and the purpose of life on earth. Yes, in a sense, we are all messengers.

However, sometimes, messages sent to us sail over our heads; other times we (human beings in general) choose to ignore them and even rationalize a path that is spiritually opposite of what we know is the right direction. Yet, God and our spiritual loved ones do not ever give up on us. Eventually, messages do get through and we gain limited understanding and acceptance of the Creator's purpose.

We make progress. We begin to view life from a more spiritual and loving perspective. Changing our behavior for the better improves the lives of all those near and dear to us as well as those who live in the distant corners of our world and probably the universe.

Being human, we often judge ourselves very critically. As I edit this manuscript doubts are ever present. I wonder about this literary effort? Is it my best? Will the words resonate in anyone's heart? Will it be a comfort to a single individual?

The introspection pendulum for all of us swings in two directions. When I compare my life to the achievements and lives of others, I fall far short of most humans. I have read of, heard of, seen, met, or known intimately, countless people more loving, compassionate, intelligent, successful, giving, talented, courageous, spiritual, generous, etc. ad en infinitum, than I. I imagine Socrates courageously risking his life daily by asking contemporaries to examine their own lives and beliefs. I stare at a photo of a young man in China standing alone before a deadly tank. My memory is full of people who have lived their lives with courage and love. Without any false humility, I can honestly say that I have never met a man, woman, or child whose personal challenges and accomplishments, I believe, I could equally face or attain.

I often conclude that I could have, should have, done more during my life and have been a better person. What are my efforts in light of all those I hold in high esteem whether they be exceptionally talented people or people courageously facing extraordinary challenges.

When the philosophical pendulum swings in the other direction, I think of the thousands, even millions of people who must cope with one form of tragedy or another, who sadly were born in a land with few opportunities or even worse, are unloved. "Why was I so lucky to be born in the U.S., been blessed with loving parents and a fine brother and sisters, wonderful wives, truly good friends, always found enjoyable work, and lived a pretty healthy and happy life?"

Eventually the pendulum swings back to center. A poem my mother gave me a long time ago comes to mind and sets everything right . . .

DESIDERATA

*Go placidly amid the noise and the haste, and
remember what peace there may be in silence.
As far as possible, without surrender, be on good
terms, with all persons. Speak your truth quietly and
clearly; and listen to others, even to the dull and
ignorant; they too have their story. Avoid loud
and aggressive persons; they are vexatious to the
spirit . . . If you compare yourself with others, you
may become vain or bitter, for always there will be
greater and lessor persons than yourself. Enjoy
your achievements as well as your plans. Keep
interested in your own career, however humble, it is
a real possession in the changing fortunes of time.
Exercise caution in your business affairs, for the
world is full of trickery. But let this not blind you to
what virtue there is; many persons strive for high
ideals, and everywhere life is full of heroism. Be
yourself. Especially do not feign affection. Neither*

be cynical about love; for in the face of all aridity and disenchantment, it is as perennial as the grass. Take kindly the counsel of the years, gracefully surrendering the things of youth. Nurture strength of spirit to shield you in sudden misfortune. But do not distress yourself with dark imaginings. Many fears are born out of fatigue and loneliness. Beyond a wholesome discipline, be gentle with yourself. You are a child of the universe no less than the trees and stars: you have a right to be here. And whether or not it is clear to you, no doubt the universe is unfolding as it should. Therefore be at peace with God, whatever you conceive Him to be. And whatever your labors and aspirations, in the noisy confusion of life, keep peace in your soul. With all its sham, drudgery and broken dreams, it is still a beautiful world. Be cheerful. Strive to be happy.

MAX EHRMANN

The words of Richard Bach, author of *JONATHAN LIVINGSTON SEAGULL*, I would like to believe, convey the spiritual philosophy of this book.

"When we come to the last moment of this lifetime and we look back across it, the only thing that's going to matter is 'What was the quality of our love?'"

It is my hope that the relating of my spiritual journey during the past five years with its detours, curves, and new vistas, may in a small way, lighten your load. The belief that the purpose of our passage on earth is to grow spiritually, brings an inner peace, helping us to bare sorrows and deeply appreciate the joys of life.

With all good wishes, love and God bless.

Richard

ADDENDUM

Dear Reader,

You may find the books listed below as interesting as I did.

WE DO NOT DIE
Martin and Romanowski

WE ARE NOT FORGOTTEN
Martin and Romanowski

OUR CHILDREN FOREVER
Martin and Romanowski

LESSONS OF THE LIGHT
Anderson and Barone

LIFE AFTER LIFE
Raymond Moody, M.D.,PH.D.

MANY LIVES, MANY MASTERS
Brien Weiss, PH.D., M.D.

ON DEATH AND DYING
Elisabeth Kubler-Ross

CONVERSATIONS WITH GOD I, II & III
Neale Donald Walsch

BIBLIOGRAPHY

Abbott, Winston. *HAVE YOU HEARD THE CRICKET'S SONG*, Inspiration House, 8th edition, 1979

Albom, Mitch. *TUESDAYS WITH MORRIE*. Doubleday, 1997

Anderson, George, and Barone, Andrew. *LESSONS OF THE LIGHT*, G.P. Putnam's Sons, 1999

Bach, Richard. *THE BRIDGE ACROSS FOREVER*, Dell Publishing, 1989

Bach, Richard. *ILLUSIONS*, Dell Publishing, Division of Bantam Doubleday, 1989

Bach, Richard. *JONATHAN LIVINGSTON SEAGULL*, The Macmillan Co., 1973

Bach, Richard. *NOTHING BY CHANCE*, Avon Books, 1969

Brinkley, Dannion. *SAVED BY THE LIGHT*, Harper Paper Backs, 1995

Campbell, Eileen. *A DANCING STAR*, Harper Collins Publishers, 1991

Canfield and Hansen. *CHICKEN SOUP FOR THE SOUL*, Health Communications, Inc., 1993

Cayce, Hugh Lynn and Edgar Cayce. *GOD'S OTHER DOOR AND THE CONTINUITY OF LIFE*, Virginia Beach, VA: A.R.E. Press, 1958

Chapin, Bruce. *THE HARDEST CHALLENGE* (Surviving the death of a spouse) Published by Teachers Insurance and Annuity Ass. N.Y., 1990

Chopra, Deepak. *THE SEVEN SPIRITUAL LAWS OF SUCCESS*, Amber-Allen Publishers, 1994

Eadie, Betty J. *EMBRACED BY THE LIGHT*, Goldleaf Press, 1992

Ehlers, Sandy McCartney, *BEYOND THE VISIBLE*, Near Water Press, 2001

Frawley, David. *FROM THE RIVER OF HEAVEN*, (Hindu and Vedic Knowledge for the Modern Age) Morson Publishing, 1990

Fulgham, Robert. *ALL I REALLY NEEDED TO KNOW I LEARNED IN KINDERGARTEN*, Ivy Books, New York, 1986

Gibran, Kahil. *THE PROPHET*, New York, Alfred A. Knopf, 1923

Grollman, Earl A. *LIVING WHEN A LOVED ONE HAS DIED*, Beacon Press, Boston MA, 1977, 1987, 1995

Guggenheim, Bill and Guggenheim, Judy. *HELLO FROM HEAVEN*, The ADC Project, 1995

Hoff, Benjamin. *THE TAO OF POOH*, Dutton Group, N.Y., 1982

Kubler-Ross, Elisabeth. *ON DEATH AND DYING*, New York: Macmillan, 1969

Lewis, C.S. *A GRIEF OBSERVED*, Bantam, 1976

THE LIGHT BEYOND, New York, Bantam Books, 1998

Lindbergh, Anne Morrow. *GIFT FROM THE SEA*, Random House Inc. and Vintage Books, 1955, 1975, 1983

LOVE BEYOND LIFE. Harper Collins, 1997

Malz, Betty. *MY GLIMPSE OF ETERNITY*, Spire Books, 1997

Martin, Joel and Patricia Romanowski. *OUR CHILDREN FOR-EVER: MESSAGES FROM THE OTHER SIDE*, Berkley Books, 1992

Moody, Raymond A. Jr., M.D., *LIFE AFTER LIFE*, Atlanta, GA: Mockingbird Books, 1975

Morgan, Marlo. *MUTANT MESSAGE DOWN UNDER*, Harper Collins Publishers, 1991, 1994

Paddison, Sara. *THE HIDDEN POWER OF THE HEART*, Planetary Publications, 1997

Praagh, James Van. *TALKING WITH HEAVEN*, Dutton, 1997

Quinn, *ISHMAEL*, Bantam/Turner Books, 1992

REUNIONS, Villard Books, New York, 1993

Rinpoche, Sogyal. *THE TIBETAN BOOK OF LIVING AND DYING*, Harper, 1997

Rodegast and Stanton. *EMMANUEL'S BOOK*, Bantam Edition, 1987

Staudacher, Carol. *A TIME TO GRIEVE*, Harper Collins, 1994

Volkman, Arthur G. *THOREAU ON MAN AND NATURE*, Peter Pauper Press, 1960

Walsch, Neale Donald. *CONVERSATIONS WITH GOD I, II & III*, Hampton Roads Publishing Co., 1995

THE WAY OF THE WIZARD, Harmony and Crown Publishers, 1995

WE ARE NOT FORGOTTEN: GEORGE ANDERSON'S MESSAGES OF HOPE FROM THE OTHER SIDE, G.P. Putham's Sons, 1991; Berkley Books, 1992

WE DO NOT DIE: GEORGE ANDERSON'S CONVERSATION WITH THE OTHER SIDE, G.P. Putham's Sons, 1998; Berkley Books, 1989

Weiss, Martin, M.D., PH.D., *MANY LIVES—MANY MASTERS*

WHERE THERE IS LIGHT, Self Realization Society, 3rd Printing, 1994

Yogananda, Paramahansa. *AUTOBIOGRAPHY OF A YOGI*, Self Realization Fellowship, twelfth Edition, 1981

FAMILY LIFE PUBLISHING
R.M. Wainwright Books

Books By Richard M. Wainwright

ALL BOOKS ARE HARDBOUND
WITH FULL COLOR ILLUSTRATIONS

TITLES AND SYNOPSIS REVIEWS

A TINY MIRACLE
ISBN: 0-9619566-0-7

Believing in something is what this read-aloud Christmas book for children and adults is all about. A small seedling is planted in the shadow of the wise old oak, so it never gets the full warmth of the sun. The tiny tree grows up smaller than the other evergreens, yet continues to believe that someday it will be chosen as a family's Christmas Tree.

The tiny tree is right... Along the way this book affirms some important values, including love between generations and kindness for others. The book's positive feelings are captured in colorful illustrations.

3 - 11 & Adults . . . 40 pages.

Direct from RMW Books $12.00
(Stores and Internet) $17.00

POOFIN
ISBN: 0-9619566-1-5

Delightful is the word that immediately comes to mind to describe **POOFIN** by Richard Wainwright. The story is one that children can relate to, the print is large, and the illustrations superb. The story is of a little cloud sent to earth at Christmas to help human beings. He has a series of humorous misadventures with the little boy who tries to straighten out the tangled results. Finally, Poofin is able to provide the little boy and the entire community with the best Christmas ever.

3 - 11 & Adults . . . 40 pages.

Direct from RMW Books $12.00
(Stores and Internet) $17.00

THE GIFT FROM OBADIAH'S GHOST
ISBN:0-9619566-2-3

OBADIAH'S GHOST is a story of overcoming fears. Tommy, the young hero, is so paralyzed by the fear of the dark that not only must he sleep with a night light on, but he cannot even bring himself to go trick or treating on Halloween. His fear is handled with great sympathy and understanding by his parents, but it is a friendly 18th century ghost who cleverly and magically helps Tommy put aside his fears.

The subject of childhood fears, particularly the fear of the dark, is treated with sensitivity and compassion. *A GIFT FROM OBADIAH'S GHOST* is a beautifully written and illustrated Halloween tale and also a story of courage.

4 - 12 & Adults . . . 40 pages.

Direct from RMW Books $12.00
(Stores and the Internet) $17.00

MOUNTAINS TO CLIMB
ISBN: 09619566-3-1

MOUNTAINS TO CLIMB (Spanish Edition)
ISBN: 09619566-5-8

MOUNTAINS TO CLIMB by Richard Wainwright and beautifully illustrated by Jack Crompton is a heartwarming story that deals with overcoming prejudice and handicaps in a positive and realistic manner. This book addresses the most pressing problems of our time—discrimination, honesty, the courage to lead, and diversity of cultures in an inspiring way. It will become a classic and should grace libraries everywhere.

It is a story of Roberto, a young Andean boy and proud owner of a one-eyed llama, who comes to live in the United States. They meet with discrimination, ridicule, and prejudice until Roberto remembers his father's advice, "in every person's life there will be many mountains to climb, but each can be conquered one step at a time." So begins the process of reaching out and helping others overcome their fears and dislike of people and things that are different from them. With Roberto's help, two physically challenged friends, are also able to find acceptance and love.

6 - 13 & Adults . . . 64 pages.

Direct from RMW Books $14.00
(Stores and the Internet) $19.00

A NEW LIFE FOR SIR CHRISTOPHER
ISBN:0-9619566-4-X

A NEW LIFE FOR SIR CHRISTOPHER is a heartwarming story of a beautiful wooden toy soldier and the effects he has on the various children who own him. We first meet Sir Christopher as a block of wood in an Indonesian rain forest. The block of wood is purchased by a master wood-carver and the doll-maker who fashions him into a beautiful Queen's Guardsman. He then travels through several families bringing joy, comfort, and sometimes courage to the children who love him. His progress, from a block of wood to a battered one-legged sea captain, is a series of adventures that will delight and captivate children and adults. Award winning author Richard Wainwright once again shows us the magic he weaves in this charming story. 4 - 12 & Adults . . . 48 pages.

Direct from RMW Books $13.00
(Stores and the Internet) $18.00

GARDEN OF DREAMS
ISBN: 0-9619566-6-6

Hopeful, positive, and timely are words that come to mind when reading Richard Wainwright's *GARDEN OF DREAMS*.

This multicultural story of Anthony's dream to improve his neighborhood is told with honesty and understanding of the problems of growing up in a racially diverse area, and the courage and hard work it takes to undertake an innovative and difficult project.

Young people will appreciate that the heroes are boys and girls who, one at a time, join together to take a simple idea and watch it grow and produce tangible results.

It is a wonderfully and beautifully illustrated story of many ethnic backgrounds coming together to add their very special talents to help fulfill the vision of a young man. 6 - 13 & Adults . . . 56 pages.

Direct from RMW Books $13.00
(Stores and the Internet) $18.00

THE CRYSTAL PALACE OF ADAMAS
ISBN: 0-9619566-8-2

THE CRYSTAL PALACE OF ADAMAS is a wonderful, beautifully written and illustrated story of Janus, a galactic pilot from the technologically advanced, yet resource depleted planet of Sagateum. Sagateum's desperate and despotic rulers wait for a message from one of their space pilots searching the universe for habitable and exploitable planets.

Janus' flight leads him to Adamas where he finds a simple, peaceful society. To his surprise, Adamians warmly welcome him to share the wonders of their planet. With his new friends Sulia, Torak, Loria, and their families, Janus begins to discover his own human emotions.

Janus' reflection and final decision revolves around societal values, ethical considerations, the use of technology, and the preservation of the natural resources of a planet. Our planet earth plays a surprising part in the outcome of the story. Richard Wainwright has written another thoughtful tale which will entrance and delight children and adults.

6 - 14 & Adults . . . 72 pages.

Direct from RMW Books $15.00
(Stores and the Internet) $20.00

NANA, GRAMPA AND TECUMSEH
ISBN: 0-9619566-7-4

Award winning author, Richard M. Wainwright's beautifully written and illustrated, *NANA, GRAMPA AND TECUMSEH* is a poignant celebration of family life. It is a story of junior high twins, Amanda and Jonathan, who lost their father in a tragic accident. The twins often spend weekends and vacations with their grandparents. Slowly they learn the miracle and richness of life from their Nana and Grampa.

Grampa takes Amanda and Jonathan to visit Tecumseh, Grampa's own tree of life. He shares with the children this strong sense of ancestry, his deep love of nature, and his extensive knowledge of Indian lore. Grampa's compassion and love of family help Amanda and Jonathan accept their father's death, their mother's new husband, and human diversity.

Grampa's final request of the twins is a last visit to Tecumseh's glen. On this journey the three generations strengthen their eternal bonds.

The young people's understanding of the web of life taught by the gentle soul of their grandfather is a story for all ages. Once again Richard Wainwright touches us all with this heartfelt story of a family sharing life's mysteries, their love for each other, and the path all living creatures must travel.

6 - 14 & Adults . . . 68 pages.

Direct from RMW Books $15.00
(Stores or Internet) $20.00

MESSENGERS
ISBN:1-928976-00-X

Award winning author Richard M. Wainwright has created yet another heart-warming and meaningful story for youngsters and adults in *MESSENGERS*.

The life of Tyler Lee Smith, an orphan of Filipino and Chinese descent, is a journey filled with many wonderful women and men who play important roles as Tyler follows his unique path.

Interwoven in the fabric of Tyler's story are human experiences and world-wide concerns including self-doubt, emotional growth, the joy of helping others, a family's unconditional love for one another, homelessness, philanthropy, adoption, the benefits and limitations of technology, and the quest for inner peace.

Readers, young and old, will be deeply moved as they recognize themselves and their personal journeys in this sensitive and profound story. Ron Walotsky's artistic talents woven throughout the story beautifully compliment the philosophy that each one of us can make a difference. We are all Messengers. 7 - 16 and Adults . . . 62 pages.

Direct from RMW Books	$15.00
(Stores and the Internet)	$20.00

CLOSER THAN WE IMAGINE
Adults . . .

Hard Cover	Direct from RMW Books	$12.50
ISBN: 1-928976-02-6	(Stores and the Internet)	$17.50
Soft Cover	Direct from RMW Books	$7.50
ISBN: 1-928976-03-4	(Stores and the Internet)	$12.50

Brochures and books may be ordered
directly by calling R.M. Wainwright Books
1 800 633 1357
or
writing

JULY – NOVEMBER	JANUARY – MAY
87 Rebecca Road	*Box 353844*
Scituate, MA 02066	*Palm Coast, FL 32135*

Praise for
RICHARD WAINWRIGHT'S BOOKS
for Children and Adults

*"ONE OF THE MOST SENSITIVE
CHILDREN'S AUTHORS WRITING TODAY.
RICHARD WAINWRIGHT'S STORIES
WILL BECOME TREASURED FRIENDS
IN A FAMILY'S COLLECTION OF BEAUTIFULLY
WRITTEN AND ILLUSTRATED BOOKS."*

DONNA FRATTO

*"RICHARD WAINWRIGHT'S WONDERFULLY
TOUCHING AND BEAUTIFULLY ILLUSTRATED
STORIES HAVE BEEN THOROUGHLY ENJOYED
BY MY GRANDCHILDREN AND MYSELF."*

MARY HIGGINS CLARK, AUTHOR

*"RICHARD WAINWRIGHT HAS
THE RARE GIFT OF BEING ABLE TO UPLIFT THE
SPIRIT OF CHILDREN AND ADULTS EQUALLY."*

JOANNE GREENE

*"FROM FANTASY, TO FEARS,
TO STORIES OF HOPE AND INSPIRATION.
RICHARD WAINWRIGHT'S BOOKS LEAD
THE YOUNG READER (and old Read-Alouder)
ON WONDERFUL WORTHWHILE JOURNEYS.
HE AND HIS ILLUSTRATORS HAVE
DONE US A GREAT SERVICE."*

DR. BRENDAN WALSH

*"RICHARD WAINWRIGHT'S STORIES
ARE SO WELL WRITTEN AND BEAUTIFULLY
ILLUSTRATED THAT THEY CAPTURE
THE IMAGINATION OF THE YOUNG
AND NOT SO YOUNG. THOSE WHO ARE LUCKY
ENOUGH TO READ RICHARD'S BOOKS
WILL BE BETTER PEOPLE FOR HAVING DONE SO.
HIS SENSITIVITY AND SKILLS BRING JOY TO ALL."*

MADELINE HAMERSLEY

*"YOUR BOOKS ARE A TREASURE!
THEY ARE NOT ONLY GREAT READING
BUT THE MESSAGES THEY CONVEY ARE
FOR ADULTS AS WELL AS KIDS."*

CLAIR AND CARL ZIRKENBACH

RICHARD M. WAINWRIGHT

Born in 1935, Richard grew up in Needham, Massachusetts spending many summers in Vermont. After a two-year hiatus in the Army, Richard completed a BA at Boston University. During the next 18 years he served as a teacher, coach, headmaster, and administrator in public and private schools.

In 1981, his first book, *A TINY MIRACLE*, was published. To Richard's wonderment, all ages loved the story and it, as well as his other books, have been reprinted many times. His stories appeal to all ages as they revolve around universal values and life's challenges. Each book takes over three years for Richard and his illustrators to complete and all of his stories have earned literary awards.

Richard's beloved wife, D'Ann, lost her battle to cancer in 1995. "She was truly the 'The wind beneath my wings.'" In September 1999, Richard married Judy Gale Smith and her wonderful family: daughter Coleby, son Doug, his wife Peggy, and their daughters, Sarah and Kelley. Judy and Richard continue to stay close to Richard and D'Ann's godchildren, Cesar, Fredy, Pablo, Mauricio and Suzie, Maria Augusta, Paquita, and Sandra Patricia.

Judy, Richard, and the family cat, Consuelo, divide their year between Scituate, Massachusetts and Palm Coast, Florida.